COPYRIGHT

WHAT EVERYONE NEEDS TO KNOW®

COPYRIGHT
WHAT EVERYONE NEEDS TO KNOW®

NEIL WEINSTOCK NETANEL

OXFORD
UNIVERSITY PRESS

OXFORD
UNIVERSITY PRESS

Oxford University Press is a department of the University of Oxford. It furthers the University's objective of excellence in research, scholarship, and education by publishing worldwide. Oxford is a registered trade mark of Oxford University Press in the UK and certain other countries.

"What Everyone Needs to Know" is a registered trademark of Oxford University Press.

Published in the United States of America by Oxford University Press
198 Madison Avenue, New York, NY 10016, United States of America.

© Oxford University Press 2018

OCT 2 6 2018 CIP data is on file at the Library of Congress
ISBN 978-0-19-994116-2 (pbk.)
ISBN 978-0-19-994114-8 (hbk.)

Hardback printed by Bridgeport National Bindery, Inc., United States of America

I dedicate this book to the memory of Peter James Brown, whom I was so very lucky to have as my father-in-law and who would have asked me a dozen questions for each question this book tries to answer.

CONTENTS

VI. Copyright in the International Arena   163

VII. "The Next Great Copyright Act": How Might Copyright Be Reformed?   175

ACKNOWLEDGMENTS

In writing this book, I have benefited greatly from substantive feedback and stylistic comments. My first thanks is to my Oxford University Press editor, James Cook. James proposed that I write this book, gave me repeated encouragement, and provided thorough, insightful edits on my manuscript.

I also owe a special debt of gratitude to Jessica Litman for her generosity and assistance. Jessica read an early version of my manuscript and provided me with a wealth of comments within days of my sending it to her. Jessica's copyright scholarship has always been an inspiration for my own. And I thank my colleague and now decades-long interlocutor David Nimmer, as well as the students in a seminar we teach together, for their very helpful comments on a much later draft.

I am also indebted to my research assistants Aaron Johnston and Colleen Parker for their research assistance and for their extremely helpful edits and substantive comments.

In addition, I thank Shalev Netanel for his comments on two drafts of my manuscript—and for challenging me to rethink everything from copyright policy to free will and determinism.

I gratefully acknowledge research support from the UCLA School of Law and UCLA Academic Senate, without which my work would not be possible.

Finally, I thank my mother, Barbara, for encouraging me to finish this book already; Adam for his abiding interest in my work (and for giving me a rest on this one!); and, most of all, my wife and life partner, Niki, for her love and support—and for sharing insights that would never have occurred to me. ‏אין כמוך!‏

INTRODUCTION

Copyright law was once an esoteric backwater, the special province of professional authors, publishers, and media companies. That's no longer the case. In our age of social media and cloud storage, we have become a copying and sharing culture. In turn, copyright law now directly implicates much of our everyday communication, work, and entertainment.

In today's world, questions about copyright abound. Do we infringe copyright when we post on YouTube a video of our two-year-old child dancing to a popular song? When we share a clip from *The Daily Show* on Facebook? When we email friends a copy of a newspaper article? When we pin on Pinterest a photo we found elsewhere on the web? When we store our music and movies in the cloud? When we subscribe to services that enable us to watch TV shows on any Internet-connected device?

These questions are highly contested. Copyright law has been unable to keep up with the explosion of new technologies for disseminating and enjoying cultural expression. Quite often, the law is unsettled or unclear. And even when the law provides a clear answer, there is still the question of whether the law should remain as it is in the face of rapid technological change. Movie studios, record labels, publishers, and major authors' associations regularly push Congress to amend our copyright law to give them more effective tools to quash widespread unlicensed copying, sharing, and remixing of copyrighted works. Technology companies, consumer advocates, and many academics vigorously resist those moves. Indeed, they generally champion peeling back copyright owner rights to allow greater leeway for personal copying and user-generated content.

Copyright, in short, has come to be immensely controversial. The 2012 battle over the proposed Stop Online Piracy Act (known as "SOPA") provides a still pertinent example. SOPA was backed by the so-called copyright industries—movie studios, record labels, print publishers, video game producers, and other content producing industries that view robust copyright protection as central to their business. SOPA would have required that Internet search, social media, payment processing, and technology companies impede individual access to foreign websites featuring allegedly infringing material. SOPA met its defeat at the hands of a popular outcry joined by Google, Facebook, Twitter, eBay, and other social media companies. It was withdrawn from consideration in Congress after some 7,000 websites coordinated a service blackout to protest the bill's purported threat to Internet freedoms.

Today, the copyright industries continue to insist that Congress must amend copyright law to target the massive online piracy that, they claim, threatens the copyright industries' economic viability. By contrast, those who led the charge against SOPA retort that the copyright industries' heavy-handed efforts to stamp out piracy would chill the free-wheeling wellspring of online creativity, commentary, and information upon which we have all come to rely.

To navigate between the opposing, equally dim prospects of ruinous piracy and heavy-handed censorship is a complex undertaking. No less daunting, even for the educated layperson, is to understand the law and conflicting policy arguments that fuel the copyright debate.

Further complicating the mix, government officials have declared that the time has come for a comprehensive revision of our copyright law. In 2013, Maria Pallante, then the Register of Copyrights, famously set out her vision for what she labeled "the next great copyright act." Since then, Congress has held no less than twenty hearings on copyright reform. Following suit, the Department of Commerce issued a white paper proposing legislation on key issues of "copyright policy, creativity, and innovation in the digital economy." And the Copyright Office has issued reports proposing legislation on matters ranging from mass digitization of books to music licensing. Academic commentators and think tanks have proffered their own blueprints, often sharply disagreeing with the vision advanced by copyright industry lobbyists.

This book provides answers to the questions about copyright law that are critical to following the copyright battles fought out in courthouses, administrative agencies, and the halls of Congress. I also untangle the heated debates regarding copyright raging in online forums, mass media, and academic and industry conferences. In so doing, I identify the combatants in the battles about copyright's present and future and examine the key arguments they present. As we shall see, the battles over copyright play out within a broader market context: Social media and digital technology are rapidly upending the business models upon which traditional news and entertainment companies—and many creators—have come to depend. I explore that phenomenon and explain how it colors the debates over copyright law.

Before we proceed, a law professor's disclaimer! My discussion is not meant as a comprehensive explanation of copyright law in all its complexity. Further, I focus on understanding the debates about copyright law and policy, not on what courts are likely to hold in any particular case. Nor do I address federal and state laws outside of copyright law, such as trademark and unfair competition laws, even though these laws might apply in certain circumstances. Finally, despite the global reach of online communication and copyright markets, my overriding focus is on U.S. copyright law and policy, although I do place U.S. copyright in a global context in Chapter VI and compare U.S. copyright law with copyright laws of other countries on several occasions. In short, while this book provides a guide to understanding copyright law and the ongoing battles that surround it, *this book is not intended as legal advice* and you should not rely on it for that purpose.

I

COPYRIGHT: WHAT IT IS AND WHAT IT IS NOT

One cannot follow the debates over copyright's present and future without understanding copyright's key doctrines and concepts. This chapter provides that understanding.

The copyright law of the United States is a product of over two hundred years of judicial decisions and congressional legislation. It spans from the Copyright Act of 1790 to our current copyright statute, the Copyright Act of 1976 (as amended numerous times since 1976). As copyright law has evolved, copyright's scope and duration have greatly expanded. In 1790, copyright holders had only the exclusive right to print and distribute books, maps, and navigational charts. And that right lasted for a maximum of twenty-eight years from publication. Today, copyright holders have more rights—including, for example, the exclusive rights to adapt, translate, and publicly perform their works. Those rights, moreover, extend to a much broader range of creative expression, including computer software, movies, music, sound recordings, and photographs. And copyrights now last for the life of the author plus seventy years.

Copyright law has also become increasingly complex and, often, counter intuitive. Lawmakers have struggled to adapt copyright law to new technologies for creating, embodying, disseminating, and consuming authors' creative works. Early sound recordings, motion pictures, broadcast, cable, satellite, home audio and video recording devices, photocopying equipment, computer programs, digital technology and the Internet have all challenged Copyright Act provisions enacted before those technologies came into being. Consequently, much of the Copyright Act is a labyrinth of detailed compromises that have been hammered out in negotiations among stakeholder industries and then enacted into law by Congress. Portions of the Copyright Act have come to resemble the tax code in their detail and impenetrability to anyone who is not an expert.

Yet other key provisions of the Copyright Act pronounce broad, open-ended, common-law standards. A key example is the provision that sets out four nonexclusive factors to guide judges in determining whether the fair use privilege applies in a particular case. Another is the codification of the "idea/expression dichotomy," the principle that copyright extends only to the form in which an author expresses her ideas, not to the ideas themselves. These provisions are simply stated. But when it comes to applying them in particular cases, they are anything but simple. Indeed, the open-ended standards can be given more precise meaning only through judges' continuing, case-by-case application. As a result, central copyright principles often defy clear definition. Indeed, they may be subject to inconsistent interpretations by different courts in different cases. Even after carefully parsing the applicable judicial precedents, one is often hard-pressed to find a definitive answer to whether certain types of creations are protected by copyright, who owns the copyright in a given work, when certain uses of copyright-protected works constitute copyright infringement, or whether a given use is a fair use.

This chapter navigates those minefields.

Copyright Basics

What is copyright?

Copyright is a set of exclusive rights that the law grants to authors of original expression. The United States Copyright

Act provides that authors of original expression shall enjoy the exclusive right to (1) copy their work; (2) distribute copies to the public; (3) prepare "derivative works" based upon their work, including translations, motion picture versions of novels, arrangements, abridgements, and the like; (4) publicly perform their work, including live performances, broadcasts, and streaming over the Internet; and (5) publicly display their work, including displaying artwork in public places and on websites. Copyright law also provides for some significant exceptions and limitations to those exclusive rights. I discuss exceptions and limitations below.

Not every use of a copyrighted work without the copyright owner's permission infringes copyright—even apart from any applicable exception or limitation. It's only a copyright infringement to use a work in a way that falls within one of the copyright owner's exclusive rights. For example, I do not infringe copyright by singing Taylor Swift's recent hit song in the shower in my home. That is a private performance, not a public one—and the copyright owner's right is to "publicly perform" the work. Nor do I infringe copyright by silently reading a bestselling novel at my local public library. Just reading a novel does not involve copying it or distributing copies to the public. But if I should suddenly jump up and, in a booming voice, read the novel out loud to startled library patrons, that would constitute a public performance. I thus would infringe the copyright in the novel unless some exception to the copyright owner's exclusive right of public performance applies.

What kind of creations does copyright protect?

Copyright law protects "original works of authorship" of any kind. These include works of literature, art, music, and choreography. They also include motion pictures, television shows, and other audiovisual works. Sound recordings, architectural works, and computer programs may enjoy copyright protection as well. Copyright law protects nonfiction as well as fiction. But entirely functional creations, such as recipes and designs of chairs, machine tools, and other utilitarian articles are typically ineligible for copyright protection except to the extent that they contain creative expression that goes beyond mere function (such as commentary accompanying a recipe that colorfully describes a dish and its history).

Beyond those basic parameters, numerous categories of creations have spawned considerable debate about whether they qualify as copyrightable works of authorship under existing law and about whether copyright protection should extend to them. These include the design of floral gardens (which, over time, may be altered by the forces of nature), fashion design (since clothes are deemed to be utilitarian articles), perfume (which is perceived by smell rather than sight or hearing), and yoga routines (which might be copyrightable choreography or a noncopyrightable method for achieving health benefits). For various reasons, movie actors' performances, restaurants' artistic display of cuisine, menu commands for operating a computer program, and golf course designs also raise questions about eligibility for copyright. So do works created by artificial intelligence computer programs endowed with machine learning capability, like a new novel in the style of an famous author generated by feeding the author's works into a computer program.

No matter what type of creation it is, a work must be "original" to qualify for copyright protection. A work is "original" if it exhibits at least a modicum of creativity. The Supreme Court has held that the alphabetical white page listings of a telephone book lack the bare minimum of creativity required for copyrightability. Most titles, slogans, basic shapes, and short phrases also lack the requisite modicum of creativity. Of course, a work that has been entirely copied from another work is not original either. Likewise, works that are created by non-human animals or that owe their shape to forces of nature are ineligible for copyright protection.

In addition to the requirement of originality, an author's creation is not protected by copyright unless and until the author fixes it in a tangible medium of expression. As I formulate the wording of this sentence in my head, it is not yet protected by copyright. But the instant I type the words, causing them to be stored in the memory of my computer, they are protected (assuming the requisite originality). Fixation can be on paper, canvas, stone, a website, or any other medium from which the work can be perceived or communicated.

Who owns the copyright?

A work's author owns the copyright in his or her work immediately upon fixing it in a tangible medium of expression. Importantly, however, authors may transfer their copyrights in whole or in part and can divide their rights by media, time, and territory. Further, according to the Copyright Act, authors may "transfer" their copyrights by assignment or exclusive license.

Hence, if I were to write a novel, I could divvy up and transfer my copyrights, whether by assignment or exclusive license, to various parties. For example, I could transfer the North American first publication rights to HarperCollins, the North American paperback rights to Bantam, the serialization rights to the Atlantic Monthly, the foreign distribution and translation rights to different publishers in various countries, the right to display and distribute my novel electronically to Amazon.com, the screenplay adaptation rights to Barry Levinson, the motion picture rights to Universal Studios, the television rights to CBS, the dramatic rights to Neil Simon, and the sequel rights to John Grisham. (I can dream, can't I?) Those parties would then each own their slice of the copyright and could enforce it against anyone (including me) who uses my novel in a way that infringes their particular right.

Most authors who want to make money from their works transfer all or part of their copyrights to companies that specialize in editing, distribution, and marketing. To create an original work is one thing. To disseminate it to the public is quite another. Companies that specialize in editing and dissemination include movie and TV studios, book publishers and newspapers, record labels, music publishers, and software companies. Very often, it is those companies—collectively referred to as the "copyright industries"—that seek to enforce the "author's" copyrights and lobby for longer and broader copyright protection.

Do creators who create works as part of their employment or on commission own the copyright?

It depends. U.S. copyright law contains a complex doctrine called "work for hire." Works that creators create within the scope of their employment or, in some instances, by commission for another person are "works made for hire." For such works, the law provides that the employer or commissioning party—not the actual creator—is the work's "author" and first copyright owner. Most creative contributions to major studio motion pictures and television shows are works made for hire, as are computer programs created by employees of software companies.

By contrast, photographs taken by freelance photographers are typically not works made for hire even if commissioned. The Copyright Act treats commissioned works differently than works created within the scope of employment. Only commissioned works that fall within one or more of nine categories set out in the Copyright Act can qualify as a work made for hire. A creative contribution that a studio commissions for a movie or TV show will qualify. A freelance photograph will generally not qualify—unless it is commissioned for use in one of the nine statutory categories, such as a movie or TV show.

Even if a commissioned work cannot qualify as a work made for hire, the creator can still assign his or her copyright to the commissioning party. By the same token, even if a work is a work made for hire, the employer or commissioning party can assign the copyright to the creator.

Joint authorship: Who owns the copyright when two or more people collaborate to create a work?

Say a lyricist and composer work together to create a song, or two screenwriters work together to create a script. Who owns the copyright in the jointly created work? Two or more people qualify as joint authors if they (1) collaborate to create a work; (2) share creative control; and (3) mutually intend to merge their creative contributions as part of inseparable or interdependent parts of that work. Some courts also require that the collaborators agree to share authorship credit to qualify as joint authors. Someone who contributes to a work but does not share creative control and/or does not receive authorship credit might not qualify as a joint author. Nor would someone who contributes only uncopyrightable concepts, ideas, or inspiration for a work.

Joint authors share the copyright. Each owns an equal share, even if one contributed more than the other. Each joint author may use the work or license its use to others without having to ask the permission of the other joint author. But the joint author who uses or licenses the joint work must provide the other joint author with an equal share of the revenues from that use or license. Those are default rules under the Copyright Act. The joint authors may agree to different arrangements regarding licensing third parties and sharing of the copyright if they so choose.

Do I have to apply for a copyright?

No. You do not have to apply for a copyright. You have copyright in your work the instant that you reduce it to some tangible form in a medium from which your work can be communicated to others for a period of more than transitory duration. As noted above, that medium might be paper, canvas, film, a CD, a smart phone, a hard drive, a website server, or any other medium from which the work may be perceived or communicated, either directly or with the aid of a machine or device.

Nevertheless, you *may* apply to register your work with the U.S. Copyright Office if you wish. There are some advantages to doing that soon after you complete your work. If someone infringes your copyright after you have registered, you may recover attorney's fees and statutory damages (which do not require that you prove actual harm). Further, if you ever want to sue someone for infringement, you must register your work prior to filing the lawsuit (unless your work originated outside the United States and you are not a U.S. national). However, you enjoy copyright protection from the moment you have fixed your work in a tangible medium of expression. Someone who copies your unregistered work without permission infringes your copyright (absent some privilege, like fair use), even though you cannot bring a copyright infringement lawsuit unless and until you register the work.

Copyright lawyers often refer to a work that is protected by copyright as "copyrighted." And in discussing whether a creation is eligible for copyright protection, they ask whether that creation is "copyrightable." Because these terms are so commonly used, I sometimes use them in this book as well. But they can be misleading because they suggest that some action must be taken to obtain copyright protection even beyond fixing the work in a tangible medium of expression.

Is there a copyright without a copyright notice?

Yes. U.S. copyright law used to require that a copyright notice be affixed to all copies of a work distributed to the public. If copies were distributed without the required notice, the work went into the public domain (with certain exceptions). But Congress abolished that requirement as of March 1, 1989, as part of U.S. adherence to the Berne Convention for the Protection of Literary and Artistic Works, which prohibits imposing formalities like notice and registration as a condition of copyright protection. (I further examine international copyright relations below.) Affixing a copyright notice is thus no longer required even if it remains standard practice for movies, books, and other works.

Beware! This means that, contrary to a common misconception, the vast bulk of text, art, video, and music posted online, whether in personal web pages or commercial sites, are protected by copyright even if not accompanied by a copyright notice. For many authors, this lack of a notice requirement for copyright protection is a blessing. It means that authors cannot inadvertently forfeit their copyright by publishing their work without a copyright notice. But it also means that massive amounts of original expression posted online are protected by copyright even if the creator gave no thought to copyright protection when creating and posting the work. The absence of formal requirements like copyright notice and registration can also greatly increase the difficulty of determining who owns the copyright in a given work. I will return to that issue below.

How long do copyrights last?

Copyrights last for a very long time, often for more than a century. Exactly how long a given work remains in copyright depends on a number of factors, including when and in what country the work was created; in what country the work was first published; whether the copyright was renewed; the type of work at issue; and when the author died. Thus, determining whether a work is still protected by copyright can require considerable factual investigation. It also requires thorough knowledge of the Copyright Act's labyrinthine provisions governing copyright term.[1]

To boil down those highly complex Copyright Act provisions to their bottom line, we can say with certainty that any work that was published prior to 1923 is in the public domain in the United States. However, works created at any time prior to 1978, going back to the dawn of human artistic expression, but first published between 1977 and 2003, will typically remain in copyright through 2047.

For works created since January 1, 1978, the Copyright Act of 1976 provides for a copyright term of the life of the author plus seventy years. However, if the work was published without the author's true name or if the work is a work-made-for-hire, the copyright term is ninety-five years from the work's first publication or 120 years from the work's creation, whichever expires first.

Prior to the Copyright Act of 1976, federal copyright protection only applied to published works. Unpublished works were protected by state common law, not federal copyright. Further federal copyright was divided into two terms. Under that two-term system, the copyright expired at the end of the initial twenty-eight-year term unless it was renewed for a second term. The two-term copyright ensured that only works for which there was continuing demand at the expiration of the initial twenty-eight-year term would remain in copyright. A Copyright Office study completed in 1960 found that the vast majority of copyrights were not renewed. Accordingly, prior to the Copyright Act of 1976, the term of copyright protection for most published works was, effectively, just twenty-eight years from first publication.

Our current Copyright Act retains that basic two-term structure for works that were created and published prior to January 1, 1978. Today, the total copyright term is ninety-five years for works published between 1923 and 1978 that were renewed at the end of their initial twenty-eight-year term. If the copyright was not renewed at the end of the initial twenty-eight-year term, the work is in the public domain. However, renewal became automatic in 1992. It no longer requires an application to the Copyright Office.

Again, the bottom line is that, as of this writing, any work that was published prior to 1923 is in the public domain in the United States. By contrast, works published between January 1, 1923 and January 1, 1964 (twenty-eight years prior to 1992), are still in copyright unless the copyright was not renewed for a second term—and/or unless the work was published without the then-required copyright notice. Renewed works first published in 1923 with a copyright notice will not enter the public domain until 2019.

Even this summary, relaying just the principal copyright term provisions, should make clear why determining whether a work is still in copyright often involves considerable investigation. To determine whether a work is still in copyright, one must know the year the work was published, and, depending on which year, whether the work was published without a copyright notice and whether the copyright was renewed. For that reason, Google and other entities engaged in the mass digitization of books in libraries' collections typically do not make a book's full text available for online viewing and downloading unless the book was first published prior to 1923 or permission has been obtained from the copyright owner. It is too expensive and time consuming even for Google to figure out whether the millions of books published in the decades following 1922 are still in copyright.

How is copyright different from patents in inventions?

Under patent law, inventors enjoy a twenty-year monopoly to make, sell, and use their inventions. To obtain a patent, an inventor must file a patent application with the United States Patent and Trademark Office. Patents are issued only for inventions that are novel, nonobvious to persons who are skilled in the field of the invention, and useful. Inventions may be devices, products, components, or processes.

So if you have a great idea for a new type of backscratcher, pharmaceutical drug, smartphone memory chip, or method of combining ingredients to make paint, that might qualify for a patent. But your invention would not qualify for copyright. Copyright does not subsist in ideas, systems, processes, or inventions. Rather, copyrights consist only of exclusive rights in original expression. Under copyright law, you might be able to prevent someone else from copying the particular text and pictures you use to describe your great idea. But you could not prevent that person from making and selling your invention. That would be the sole province of patent law.

In addition, copyright infringement requires actual copying. You do not infringe copyright if, without copying, you create a work that just happens to be identical to an existing work. By contrast, you infringe a patent by making the same invention that is subject to someone else's patent even if you invented it completely independently, without knowing that someone else has already invented it and obtained a patent. Hence, although copyrights last much longer than patents, patents provide a far more robust monopoly.

Copyrights and patents can sometimes overlap. For example, a computer program that embodies a novel and nonobvious method of software operation might qualify as a patentable invention as well as a copyrightable literary work. However, copyright doctrine aims to prevent the use of copyright as a back door to protecting inventions that might not meet the strict requirements for patentability. For example, the Copyright Act explicitly provides that in no case does copyright protection extend to any procedure, process, method of operation, system, concept, or principle. The underlying principle is that these items should obtain intellectual property protection only if they are sufficiently novel and nonobvious to qualify for a patent. Likewise, copyright law provides limited protection for the design of useful articles—articles that have some intrinsic utilitarian function, such as clothing, furniture, lamps, and smartphones. A useful article enjoys copyright protection only if its design features stand on their own as a work of art if imagined apart from the functional aspects of the article's design.

There is much debate about patent law and policy. Issues range from whether newly created life forms should be patentable subject matter to whether the Patent Office issues too many patents for inventions that are not truly novel and nonobvious. Some of the policy arguments raised in patent debates have relevance for debates about copyright law. Certainly, at a general abstract level, both ask whether innovation and creativity are best served by strong, proprietary rights in intellectual creations or rather by relative freedom to share and build upon others' intellectual creations. But there are some significant differences between copyright and patent doctrine, subject matter, industries, and markets. So it is important not to conflate them.

Finally, patent law also provides for exclusive rights in aesthetic elements of industrial design. These are called "design patents," as distinguished from "utility patents" granted for useful inventions. Design patents may sometimes overlap with copyright protection for the aesthetic features of useful articles. But like utility patents, design patents may be infringed even by someone who did not copy from the patented design. Recent years have seen an explosive growth in the issuance of design patents as the Patent Office and the courts have lowered the threshold for obtaining them.

How is copyright different from trademark?

Trademarks are words, logos, images, sounds, or other symbols that identify the source of a good or service. The word "Apple" serves as a trademark for Apple, Inc.'s computers, mobile devices, and iTunes music and video distribution service. So does Apple's stylized graphic of an apple with a bite taken out of it. Trademark law forbids the use of someone else's trademark in a way that confuses consumers regarding the source of a good or service or that dilutes the power of a famous trademark to connote a particular source. If I were to manufacture and sell my own computers with the word "Apple" emblazoned on them, consumers would be misled into thinking that my computers were manufactured by or under contract for Apple, Inc. and that they are subject to Apple's quality control and consumer warranties. As a result, consumers would be harmed, and Apple's reputation would suffer.

Trademark law does not prevent anyone from using a word that serves as a company's trademark in a context that does not cause consumer confusion or dilution. I can sing a song containing the line, "An apple doesn't fall far from the tree" without infringing Apple, Inc.'s trademark. Likewise, a car dealer can call itself "Apple Sports Imports" and a farmer named Jones can sell "Farmer Jones' Apples." Consumers would not think that Apple, Inc. is the source of those goods. Nor would they think that the car dealer or farmer are somehow affiliated with Apple, Inc.

Unlike copyright law, trademark law does not require that a word or other symbol must be creative in order to qualify for a trademark. Obviously, Apple, Inc. did not create the word "apple." Rather, trademark law requires that, to be a trademark, the word "Apple" must distinguishe Apple, Inc.'s products and services from products and services produced by other manufacturers in similar lines of business. Also unlike copyright, a trademark may remain in force indefinitely so long as it continues to be used to identify the source of a good or service.

Trademarks and copyrights can sometimes overlap. For example, the cartoon image of Mickey Mouse is protected both by copyright law as a creative graphic work and by trademark law as a source identifier for Disney books, movies, and merchandise. Even when the copyright in the Mickey Mouse character expires, Mickey Mouse can continue to serve as a trademark for Disney goods and services. When that happens, a graphic of Mickey Mouse may appear within movies, videogames, and books so long as it is not used in a manner that might confuse consumers into thinking that Disney is the sponsor.

Is copyright a property right?

Whether copyright can properly be called a "property right" is subject to fierce debate, a debate that extends back to the eighteenth century. We tend to think of property rights as rights of absolute individual dominion. In the popular imagination, if something is ours, we may do with it what we want. No one else may intrude or interfere. For that reason, those who favor expansive copyrights have repeatedly characterized copyright as "property." If authors have property rights in their creative expression, they should have broad exclusive rights, covering many different uses of their works and subject to only the narrowest of exceptions.

By contrast, those who favor narrowly tailored copyrights,. punctuated by robust exceptions and limitations, cast copyright as a limited monopoly, tax on readers, special reward, trade regulation, or government entitlement, not a right of property. For example, in propounding a fair use privilege for consumers to record television programs for later viewing, the Supreme Court stated that "[t]he monopoly created by copyright . . . rewards the individual author in order to benefit the public." The Court further explained that "there are situations . . . in which strict enforcement of this monopoly would inhibit the very 'Progress of Science and useful Arts' that copyright is intended to promote."[2]

Both sides are partly correct. Copyright is a set of exclusive rights in an intangible thing, an original work of authorship, that is enforceable against anyone. In that sense, copyright has characteristics we typically associate with property rights. But unlike property rights in tangible things, copyrights are not meant to secure the owner's exclusive possession and enjoyment. Rather the federal government grants copyrights to authors in order to promote the public benefit. Copyright provides an economic incentive for the creation and dissemination of works of knowledge, opinion, and imagination that we all enjoy.

Moreover, until enactment of the Copyright Act of 1976, copyrights far more resembled a limited government monopoly than what we normally think of as a property right in a tangible object or in land. Copyrights lasted for a much shorter time than today: just twenty-eight years with a rarely exercised right to renew for another twenty-eight years at the end of the first term. In addition, federal copyright protection was generally available only for published works and was conditional upon affixing a copyright notice to copies distributed to the public. The author was also required to deposit two copies of the work with the U.S. Copyright Office so that the public could have free access to it in the Library of Congress.

For most purposes it should not matter whether copyright is a property right. Notwithstanding our idealized image of property as a right of absolute dominion, property rights come in all shapes and sizes—and are subject to numerous constitutional, regulatory, and common-law limitations. So merely to classify copyright as property—or, conversely, to deny that moniker—actually tells us very little about copyright's proper scope and duration. Nonetheless, labeling copyright as property carries significant symbolic force. The notion that if copyright is "property," it should resemble a perpetual, absolute property right has repeatedly infused judicial proceedings, legislative enactments, and public debate about copyright law.

In recent years, for example, some authors and copyright industry spokespersons have invoked the "copyright is property" trope to insist that to copy without permission any portion of a song, text, or movie, even to build upon it to create a new work, is nothing short of "stealing" and thus should be subject to harsh legal sanctions and moral opprobrium. Likewise, copyright industry lobbyists apply to copyright what they claim (incorrectly) is the universal property law rule that any interference with possession absent the property owner's prior consent is a trespass. The analogous rule, in their view, is that copyright exceptions and limitations should be narrowly construed. Indeed, they argue, given that copyright is a property right, no one may copy, display, or perform a copyrighted work without the copyright owner's advance permission, even when advance permission is impossible to obtain because the copyright owner is unknown.

Do authors have a constitutional right to copyright protection?

No. The U.S. Constitution grants Congress the power and authority to enact a copyright law. But it does not require that Congress enact such a law. Nor does it give authors a constitutional right to copyright protection.

Unlike legislatures in many other countries, Congress does not have the general power to enact legislation on any subject of its choosing. Rather, Congress only has the legislative powers enumerated in the Constitution. The so-called enumerated powers include, among others, the power to regulate interstate commerce, levy taxes, spend the money raised from taxes for general welfare, and establish bankruptcy laws. The enumerated powers also include those granted to Congress under Article I, Section 8, of the Constitution. That clause of the Constitution—the so-called Copyright and Patent Clause—gives Congress the power "To promote the Progress of Science and useful Arts, by securing for limited Times to Authors and Inventors the exclusive Right to their respective Writings and Discoveries." The Framers of the Constitution evidently believed that without that clause Congress would have no authority to enact a copyright law.

Notably, the Copyright and Patent Clause seems to limit Congress' power in certain ways. For example, copyrights must be for "limited Times." And copyrights must be granted to "Authors," which the Supreme Court has interpreted to mean that Congress has no authority to grant copyright protection to works that lack even a modicum of creativity.

Even though the Constitution does not require Congress to enact a copyright law, once Congress has enacted a law that grants copyrights to authors, those who own existing copyrights under that law *might* have a constitutional right against being deprived of their rights without compensation from the government. The Constitution provides that "private property [shall not] be taken for public use, without just compensation." As noted in the previous question, whether copyrights qualify as "property" is a matter of debate. But if copyrights do qualify as "private property" under the Constitution, those who own that property might be entitled to compensation for the taking of their property if Congress were to decide to abolish copyright protection for all existing works and to dedicate those works to the public domain. That hypothetical poses complicated questions of constitutional law involving government takings of property that I cannot address here. But even if current copyright owners might have rights against uncompensated takings, no author has a constitutional right to copyright protection for works that he or she might create in the future.

What is the Copyright Office?

The U.S. Copyright Office is a department within the Library of Congress. The head of the Copyright Office is called the "Register of Copyrights."

The Copyright Office acts somewhat like a land title registry: It processes and records copyright registrations and notices of transfers of copyright ownership. In so doing, the Copyright Office promulgates and implements policies regarding which types of creations are eligible for copyright and which are not.

The Copyright Office also administers several so-called statutory licenses. These arise from Copyright Act provisions that allow certain uses of copyrighted works without the copyright holder's permission so long as the user pays a royalty at the rate set by the Copyright Royalty Board, a body of administrative judges appointed by the Librarian of Congress. Within that framework, the Register of Copyrights may provide advisory opinions to the Copyright Royalty Board and review the Board's determinations of statutory royalty rates for legal error.

In addition, the Copyright Office issues various regulations. For example, pursuant to the Digital Millennium Copyright Act of 1998 (DMCA), the Copyright Office administers a triennial rulemaking concerning the circumvention of technological protection measures. As explained below, the DMCA prohibits the circumvention of digital encryption and other technological protection measures that enable copyright owners to control access to copyrighted material. But in its rulemaking, the Copyright Office may temporarily exempt some users from that prohibition if it finds, for example, that circumvention is necessary to engage in fair use.

In addition to those administrative responsibilities, the Copyright Office plays an important role in copyright policymaking. It conducts studies and produces reports for Congress on a broad array of copyright law and policy issues. It also provides support for executive branch agencies regarding what the Copyright Office terms "trade and antipiracy initiatives."

In its policymaking capacity, the Copyright Office has stood at the center of several legislative initiatives in the area of copyright law, including the Copyright Act of 1976. In recent years, it has issued reports and conducted hearings regarding orphan works (works for which the copyright owner is unknown and cannot readily be identified), music licensing, statutory licensing, mass digitization, small claims courts for copyright infringement lawsuits, moral rights, Internet service provider liability for users' infringements, and other matters.

The Copyright Office has drawn repeated criticism from copyright critics. Critics argue that the Office consistently takes positions that favor the copyright industries rather than representing the public interest as a whole.[3] A prime lightening rod of that criticism was the Copyright Office's endorsement of the Stop Online Piracy Act, which was backed by the copyright industries but went down to defeat in a public outcry led by social media and technology companies.

Critics also cite a bias-inducing "revolving door." Copyright Office legal and policy staff include former lawyers for authors' associations and copyright industries. And Copyright Office staff regularly leave to work for copyright industries. For example, Maria Pallante, who served as Register of Copyrights from 2011 to 2016, had previously held leadership positions with the Authors Guild and National Writers Union and, upon leaving the Copyright Office, was appointed president and CEO of the Association of American Publishers.

The Copyright Office has not formally responded to such criticism. Nor would one expect a government agency to do so.

It is difficult to measure objectively the charges of bias levied against the Copyright Office. Whether one agrees with the charges likely depends on where one sits in ongoing debates over copyright law and policy. At the very least, Copyright Office reports and policy positions must be read critically rather than accepted on their face.

That healthy skepticism of Copyright Office positions surfaces in judicial rulings as well. Some courts give weight to the Copyright Office's expertise in copyright matters. But courts have sometimes declined to follow Copyright Office interpretations of various aspects of copyright law.

Copyright Infringement

What is copyright infringement?

Recall that copyright law accords copyright owners a set of exclusive rights in creative expression. These include the exclusive right to make or publicly distribute copies of a copyrighted work, publicly perform or display the work, and prepare derivative works based on the work. You potentially infringe copyright if your use of a copyrighted work falls within any of those exclusive rights and you use the work without the copyright owner's permission. However, you might not infringe if your use of the copyrighted work qualifies for an exception or limitation to the copyright owner's rights, such as fair use. I explain copyright exceptions and limitations below.

What if I copy a small part of your work or if I change it? Do I still infringe your copyright?

It can be infringing to copy a small part of someone else's work or even to build on someone else's work in creating a new one.

Copyright does not merely give the copyright owner the exclusive right to make exact copies of an entire work. The copyright owner also has the exclusive right to copy discrete parts of a work. For example, a songwriter may prevent another from digitally sampling a line from his song and a novelist may prevent another from copying even a single paragraph from her book—unless that copying qualifies for a defense to infringement like fair use, discussed below.

In addition, the copyright owner's exclusive right to copy includes making what are often called "nonliteral copies." These include copying a novel's or film's storyline, events, settings, and characters, even without copying any of the work's literal text or dialogue. What's more, the copyright owner's exclusive right to make derivative works includes the right to make abridgements, sequels, adaptations in other media, and other versions that incorporate some of the work's copyright-protected expression.

Say I write a novel that borrows from yours but also contains much of my own original expression. If you sue me for copyright infringement, I cannot defend merely by demonstrating how much of your work I did not copy or how much of my work is not a copy of yours. It matters only what I did copy. So long as I copy sufficient copyrightable expression from your work, I infringe your copyright, unless I can successfully assert a defense to infringement such as fair use. And that's the case even if my copying is "nonliteral."

As a result, the battles over copyright are only partly about out-and-out copyright piracy—whether and how copyright owners should be entitled to enforce their copyrights more effectively to thwart those who slavishly copy and distribute entire works for a profit. Nor do the debates focus entirely on consumer downloading and copying of entire works for personal enjoyment. Rather, the battles over copyright also center on issues of "follow-on authorship." In other words, should today's authors have leeway to use existing works as raw material for new creative expression? Should rap artists have to clear rights for each digital sample they include in their songs? Should documentary filmmakers have to obtain permission to include period-piece art and music in their films when those works are still in copyright? Should appropriation artists be able to "pay homage to" or "quote from" existing paintings, advertisements, or photographs by replicating those works in their art? Should authors be free to write sequels and satires of existing novels—and should it matter whether the author is an amateur fan fiction writer or a professional? Should copyright law tolerate the unlicensed remixes and mash-ups that populate YouTube, Instagram, BuzzFeed, and other such sites? Virtually all great—and not-so-great—writers, composers, and artists borrow from previous genres and works to some extent, often without permission. The question of whether copyright law should allow that practice remains a contentious issue among scholars, policymakers, and creators themselves.

Does copyright law prevent you from "stealing my idea"?

Copyright does not protect ideas. Nor does it protect facts. Rather copyright protects only the literal or artistic form in which an author expresses ideas or facts.

As far as copyright law is concerned, anyone is free to copy the basic ideas found in novels or screenplays. For example, the general idea of a tragic romance between two teenagers belonging to warring families is free for the taking. However, you may not copy the author's particular expression of an idea: including the author's plot, characters, and dialogue. Similarly, anyone may copy the facts conveyed in a newspaper article or documentary film. You just may not copy the particular words or scenes that convey those facts. Likewise, anyone may make a cubist painting that depicts musical instruments. But you may not copy the particular composition, setting, and subject of Picasso's *Mandolin and Guitar*.

This basic tenet of copyright law is often referred to as the "idea/expression dichotomy." Ideas and facts are free for the taking, no matter how novel or profound. Original expression is protected by copyright.

While the distinction between idea and fact versus expression is easy to state in principle, it can be quite difficult to determine when an alleged infringer has copied the author's protectable "expression" rather than only the author's unprotectable "idea." The reason is that, as noted in the previous question, it may be infringing even to make a nonliteral copy of expression, such as copying a novel's storyline, without copying or closely paraphrasing any passages or dialogue — and it is often unclear whether nonliteral copying is copying of "expression" or copying of "idea." There is no generally applicable rule that defines at what level of abstraction nonliteral copying becomes copying expression rather than idea. As Judge Learned Hand once put it: "Obviously, no principle can be stated as to when an imitator has gone beyond copying the 'idea,' and has borrowed its 'expression.' Decisions must therefore inevitably be ad hoc."[4]

Consider, for example, the Broadway musical *West Side Story* and Shakespeare's *Romeo and Juliet*. *West Side Story* is meant to be a modern, musical adaptation of *Romeo and Juliet*. It does not copy any of Shakespeare's dialogue, actual characters, stage directions, costumes, or settings. But *West Side Story* does copy certain plot elements from Shakespeare's tragedy and transposes them from Renaissance Italy to a blue-collar neighborhood in 1950s New York City. For example, like *Romeo and Juliet*, *West Side Story* features two young lovers from warring groups, culminating in tragic death (in *Romeo and Juliet* of both lovers, while in *West Side Story* one lover) as a result of a misunderstanding, followed by the characters' recognition of the need to end the violent feud.

If *Romeo and Juliet* were protected by copyright today would *West Side Story* infringe? It's tough to say. As Judge Hand has taught us, the decision would inevitably be ad hoc. Some courts and commentators might posit that the basic plot elements that *West Side Story* copies from *Romeo and Juliet* are uncopyrightable ideas. But others might hold that *West Side Story* constitutes a "nonliteral copy" of *Romeo and Juliet*'s copyrightable expression. That very uncertainty means that if *Romeo and Juliet* were in copyright today, *West Side Story* might never be produced. Who would risk being sued by Shakespeare's literary estate?

What if I copy your work only for myself or share my copy with others for free?

We regularly use our computers and mobile devices to copy copyrighted expression. We might save a newspaper article from a website for later reading. Or we copy music from our computer onto our cloud storage folder to save hard drive space or to be able to listen to it from multiple devices. We also copy photos, articles, and videos and share them on social media sites.

Is that copying and sharing legal? That question is hotly contested. Some consumer advocates argue that individuals do not infringe copyright when they make noncommercial copies of copyright-protected works solely for their own personal use—and that that is how it should be. By contrast, copyright industries and author organizations generally insist that the law requires the copyright owner's permission for all copying. Granted, copyright owners have willingly tolerated a great deal of unlicensed personal copying thus far. But the copyright industries and author organizations still insist that such personal copying is infringing. In their view, you must receive the copyright owner's permission to transfer your music and videos from one device to another, or to cloud storage, even if you have purchased that content. Indeed, copyright industries have expressed interest in monetizing such multi-device access as a new source of revenue.

Until the advent of consumer copying technology, personal copying was a non-issue. No copyright owner much cared if a few isolated individuals took the time and trouble to manually copy a novel, music notation, or painting for their own personal use. But personal computers and mobile devices can make digital copies that are indistinguishable from the original. And the Internet makes it easy to share those homemade copies the world over. That has radically changed the equation. For the first time, noncommercial copying and sharing, done on a massive scale by millions of individuals, has the potential to undermine sales of copyright-licensed copies and streaming.

Concurrently, the proliferation of devices through which we can read, hear, or watch cultural products has created a new demand for digital copies of products that we have purchased. We want the convenience of being able to access our e-books, music, movies, and television programs on multiple devices. Likewise, our social media invite us to share with others copyrighted works that we find online. That copying and sharing has become a routine part of online conversation for millions of Internet users.

Which side is right? What does current copyright law provide with respect to personal and noncommercial copying? Here, too, there is no clear answer. Copyright laws of some other countries provide for a private copying exception from copyright—and, in return, impose a levy on copying equipment and media, with the proceeds allocated to authors. But, except for a couple narrow instances, the U.S. Copyright Act has no such private copying exception. Reading just the language of the Act, a copyright owner has the broad, exclusive right to copy his or her work. Copying without permission would seem to be infringing even if you just make a copy for yourself without sharing it with anyone else at all. Nor is there an express exception for noncommercial sharing.

Nonetheless, copying for personal use or sharing in social media might, at least sometimes, qualify as a noninfringing fair use. (Some personal copying, such as photocopying a New Yorker cartoon to put on your refrigerator door, might also qualify as a "de minimis" use, a use so trifling that it is excused under copyright law.) Below I explain fair use and examine judicial rulings regarding fair use and personal copying.

Is copyright infringement the same as plagiarism?

The terms "copyright infringement" and "plagiarism" are sometimes used interchangeably, even by judges. But they are not the same.

Plagiarism means copying someone else's expression or idea without identifying that person as the source of that expression or idea. By contrast, copyright law prohibits copying someone's original expression (but not ideas), regardless of whether the source is properly identified. Further, unlike copyright infringement, to commit plagiarism is only to violate a social or ethical norm. It is not a violation of the law per se (even if in a commercial context, a plagiarist might sometimes face liability for fraud, false advertising, or unfair competition).

Say you write a book presenting your novel theory that even monkeys ostracize those who copy another's creation without permission. I commit plagiarism if I write a scholarly article presenting that same theory as if it were my own, without attributing it to you. But I would not infringe your copyright unless I also copied or closely paraphrased your expression—the literal formulation in which you conveyed your theory. Conversely, no matter how much of your book I copy, I do not commit plagiarism so long as I credit you as the source for what I have copied. But if I copy and distribute your book without your permission, I would infringe your copyright even if I correctly identified you as the book's sole author.

Copyright Licensing and Permissions

Whom do I need to ask for permission to use a copyrighted work?

You typically need the copyright owner's permission to make a use of a copyrighted work that falls within any of copyright's exclusive rights unless your use qualifies for an exception to copyright like fair use.

But it can be difficult to determine who is the person you need to ask for permission. Recall that neither copyright registration nor a copyright notice is required for a work to be protected by copyright. In addition, the copyright in a work is often sliced and diced, with various rights assigned to different parties. And those rights may be further divided by the time period of exclusivity, distribution media, and territory. Copyright transfers may be recorded with the Copyright Office, and there are some benefits to doing so. But like registration and notice, there is no requirement that a copyright transfer be recorded. As a result, there is often no public record of who owns the copyright—or, more accurately, who owns the particular right that covers the use for which you might need a copyright license. (A "copyright license" is the legal term for the rights holder's permission. An "exclusive license" means that no one but the licensee has permission; a "nonexclusive license" means that others might have permission to use the copyrighted work in the same way.)

Copyrights' long duration greatly exacerbates the problem of locating the party from whom a copyright license must be obtained. Copyrights can often outlive the author, the author's immediate heirs, and even the publishing company or studio that initially released the work to the public. Further, copyright transfer agreements do not always make clear whether rights to exploit the work in new technological media unknown at the time of the agreement are included in the transfer of rights or are retained by the author. That ambiguity may pose a quandary for exploiting the work in later developed technological media. For example, does a book publishing contract signed in 1960 give the publisher the right to issue an e-book version in 2010? Does a synchronization license (a license to include a musical composition in a movie or TV show) signed in 1960 give the studio the right to sublicense Netflix to stream over the Internet the movie that incorporates that song?

In short, if you want to make such a digital use of a predigital work, you must first find the original assignment or license.

Then you must try to figure out whether the author assigned rights to exploit the work in "any technological media, now known or later developed." You then must try to identify and locate the current copyright owner of the relevant digital rights.

Why is music licensing so complicated?

As anyone who works in the music industry can attest, music licensing is exceedingly complicated. The reason is that the dissemination of recorded music involves multiple copyrighted works, exclusive rights, copyright owners, and statutory license regimes. In my answer to this question, I unpack the basics of music licensing. We return to some of the specifics in later questions.

Recorded music

Recorded music typically includes three separate components, each of which is entitled to protection under the Copyright Act. First, there is the musical work. The musical work includes both the musical composition and any accompanying lyrics. Second, there is the sound recording. The sound recording is the product of the sound engineer's capture, mixing, and editing of a particular performance of the musical work in the recording studio or on stage. Third, there is the live performance of the musical work in the recording studio or on stage. The Copyright Act provides that no one may publicly communicate or record a live music performance without the performers' permission. Nor may anyone distribute copies of such a recording without the performers' permission. Congress granted music performers those rights in their live performances primarily to combat bootleg recordings of concert performances. But the rights apply to performances in recording studios as well.

Timing

To add to that complexity, Congress added protection for each component—the musical work, sound recording, and live music performance—at different times. Musical works have enjoyed copyright protection since well over a century before enactment of the Copyright Act of 1976. Congress expressly granted copyright protection to musical works in 1831. By contrast, Congress extended copyright protection to sound recordings only in 1972. Sound recordings produced prior to February 15, 1972, are protected only by state law, if at all—although Congress is now considering legislation that would retroactively extend federal copyright protection to pre-1972 recordings. Finally, Congress granted music performers rights in live music performances only as of December 8, 1994. But unlike copyright protection for sound recordings, music performers' rights to prevent the sale of bootleg recordings apply to recordings made prior to that date as well as to more recent recordings.

Ownership of rights

Tracing the ownership of the rights in musical works, sound recordings, and live performances is also a complex undertaking. Composers and lyricists who collaborate in creating new songs are typically joint authors of the copyright in those musical works. Further, members of a singer-songwriter rock band might each make sufficient contributions to composing a song such that several qualify as joint authors. The default rule is that any joint author may grant a copyright license for the joint work, but the joint authors may agree by contract that all must agree to such a license. In addition, songwriters often assign their copyrights to a music publisher, tasked with marketing and administering the commercial exploitation of the song. Finally, rights in musical works are typically administered by collective rights management organizations on behalf of songwriters and music publishers. I discuss such organizations below.

The authors of the sound recording are generally understood to be both the sound engineer and the recording artists (the singers and musicians who performed the songs that were recorded). But the record label that organized the recording of the music typically owns the copyright in the resulting sound recording, either because the label takes assignment of the copyright from its authors or because the sound recording is created as a work made for hire. Somewhat similarly, given that the recording artists explicitly or implicitly give permission to the record label to record their live music performance in the recording studio, the record label is typically understood to have the right to distribute copies of the recording and to license others to distribute copies of the recording.

The rights that apply to each type of work

In addition, different rights attach to each the musical work, sound recording, and live music performance. Accordingly, someone who wants to make recorded music available to the public must obtain licenses for different rights and different types of works, depending on how the music is being made available.

The copyright in a musical work includes the exclusive rights to make and distribute copies and phonorecords of the work. A "copy" of a musical work is the fixation of the musical work in sheet music or in the sound track of a movie or other audiovisual work. A "phonorecord" of a musical work is a material object in which only the sounds of a performance of that musical work are fixed and from which those sounds can be perceived, reproduced, or otherwise communicated. A record album, whether it be vinyl or a digital CD, is a phonorecord of each musical work that appears in the album. Digital files of recordings of musical works, such as those available for download on iTunes, are also treated as phonorecords under the Copyright Act.

The copyright in the musical work also includes the exclusive right to publicly perform the work. Under the Copyright Act, to "publicly perform" a work includes live performances, broadcasts, and online streaming.

By contrast, when Congress extended copyright to sound recordings, it excluded the right of public performance from those copyrights. That is why radio stations that broadcast over the airwaves do not need to ask permission from the record label to broadcast a sound recording. Rather, radio stations must obtain permission only from the owners of the copyrights in the musical works that the stations wish to broadcast.

However, in 1995 Congress provided for a new, narrow public performance right: the right to publicly perform sound recordings by means of a digital audio transmission—including digital satellite radio and what is today referred to as online streaming. Congress did so to address the concern of record labels and recording artists that online music streaming would supplant the market for sales of record albums. But under the Copyright Act, the record labels now enjoy an *exclusive* digital performance right only against interactive streaming services, those that enable consumers to choose exactly which songs they wish to hear. For services like Internet and satellite radio, where consumers cannot determine the exact playlist, Congress has carved out a statutory license regime, which I discuss below.

Finally, as noted above, live music performers have the exclusive right to record and publicly communicate their live performance, and to make and distribute copies (music accompanied by a series of related images) and phonorecords (audio only) of their performance. As with sound recordings, live music performers do not have the exclusive right to publicly perform recordings of their performance. Hence Apple must have the performers' permission to sell downloads through iTunes of recordings of live performances made in the recording studio or at a live concert. That permission is typically granted by the record label. By contrast, radio stations do not need to obtain performers' permission to broadcast a recording of the performance. A radio station would need the performers' permission only if it were broadcasting a live performance, such as a concert.

Compulsory licenses

Adding to the complexity of music licensing, some aspects of music licensing are governed by compulsory license regimes instead of the copyright owner's exclusive rights. In those instances, the copyright owner has no right to prevent the use of the work so long as the user pays the fee set by a court or administrative judicial body. I discuss compulsory licenses below, so I will not go into detail here. Suffice it to say that most public performances of musical works are subject to compulsory licenses pursuant to the terms of judicially enforced antitrust decrees. In addition, Congress has provided for compulsory licenses in the Copyright Act for making and distributing cover recordings and other phonorecords of musical works that have previously been recorded and distributed to the public. That compulsory license applies to providing digital downloads of songs as well as to selling songs on CDs. Finally, as noted above, Congress provided for a compulsory license for the digital transmission of sound recordings by Internet and satellite radio. Music licensing in all those areas entails repeated hearings before the judicial and administrative bodies that oversee the compulsory license and determine the fees to be paid.

What are collective rights management organizations?

Collective rights management organizations enable authors and other copyright holders to band together to license certain uses of copyrighted works and to enforce copyrights against unauthorized users. For example, the American Society of Composers, Authors and Publishers (ASCAP) enforces and licenses rights to publicly perform music on behalf of its more than 600,000 songwriter and music publisher members. ASCAP was established in the early twentieth century as a means for songwriters and music publishers to ensure that bars, restaurants, and concert halls paid royalties for live music performances. Today, ASCAP also licenses radio stations and music streaming services and brings lawsuits against those who publicly perform ASCAP members' music without an ASCAP license. ASCAP licenses over 10 million songs and collects royalties on a trillion performances each year. ASCAP also tracks a sample of songs that are performed and distributes royalty proceeds to its members, roughly in accordance with the number of performances of each song.

ASCAP typically grants "blanket licenses," in other words a license to perform any song in ASCAP's repertoire in return for paying a license fee calculated as a percentage of the licensee's revenues. Broadcast Music, Inc., (BMI), the Society of European Stage Authors and Composers (SESAC), and Global Music Rights (GMR) similarly license public performance rights for music on behalf of their members. Other collective rights management organizations operating in the United States include Sound Exchange, which licenses digital public performance rights on behalf of record labels; the Harry Fox Agency, which licenses the right to make and distribute phonorecords (*i.e.*, audio only recordings) of musical compositions, including digital downloads; and the Copyright Clearance Center, which licenses universities and corporations the right to copy from books and articles and to show motion pictures and television programs within those organizations.

Collective rights management organizations provide significant benefits for their members, even if songwriters sometimes complain that their organization diverts too large a share of royalty payments for overhead. Collective licensing also benefits users. It enables them to obtain the licenses they need from a single source rather than having to locate individual copyright owners and transact for numerous individual licenses.

Nevertheless, the advent of digital technology has posed significant challenges for collective rights management organizations. Digital technology greatly enhances rights holders' capability of tracking uses of their copyrighted works and negotiating individual licenses with prospective users. As a result, some large rights holders—principally major music publishers—have less need to be represented by a collective licensing organization. Further, the emergence of new digital media calls into question whether uses in those media are and should be covered by traditional collective licensing agreements.

Challenges to the collective licensing system have arisen with particular force in the area of music performance licensing, where ASCAP and BMI together represent the vast majority of songwriters and music publishers. ASCAP and BMI have operated under the terms of antitrust consent decrees since 1941. The decrees effectively impose on the organizations a judicially supervised compulsory license. ASCAP and BMI must license the songs in their respective repertoires to any user under reasonable terms, and any aggrieved user may apply for relief from the court that presides over the applicable antitrust consent decree. The basic rationale behind the antitrust consent decrees is that ASCAP's and BMI's monopoly control over the vast majority of songs would enable them to engage in illegal price fixing unless they are required to license any user at reasonable rates.

Recently, the Antitrust Division of the Justice Department opened a review of the ASCAP and BMI consent decrees. It sought to determine if the decrees still make sense in the digital era, especially given that music streaming services like Spotify, Apple, and Pandora arguably have the market power to counter that of ASCAP and BMI. The Justice Department concluded in August 2016 that the consent decrees have "well served music creators and music users for decades and should remain intact."[5]

Nevertheless, some songwriters and music publishers have pushed for the right to negotiate individual licenses, presumably for higher fees, while still benefitting from membership in ASCAP or BMI. In particular, two leading music publishers, Universal Music and Sony/ATV, have sought to withdraw their songs from ASCAP for the limited purpose of licensing digital performances in individual negotiations with webcasters and other music Internet sites, including Pandora, YouTube, and Spotify. The music publishers insist that, given the development of digital platforms for licensing and tracking online music performances, they no longer need ASCAP to administer digital performance licenses on their behalf. The publishers, no doubt, also wish to hold out for higher license fees than would otherwise be permitted by the presiding anti-trust court. However, the court held that ASCAP members may not selectively withdraw their songs from ASCAP for certain uses or licensees only. A songwriter or publisher who chooses to be a member of ASCAP must give ASCAP permission to license that ASCAP member's songs for all uses and licensees, as part of ASCAP's repertoire.

Why can't everyone who wants to use someone else's work just get a copyright license?

As we have just seen, it can be difficult to determine who owns the rights that must be licensed. Moreover, determining who owns the rights is just the beginning. In many new media markets, it can be exceedingly complex and costly for new media companies to obtain the multiple copyright licenses they need to make cultural works available online. That is true even when some licenses are provided by collective rights management organizations.

I have just discussed music licensing, so let's take that as an example. Consider Spotify. Spotify is a commercial music streaming and download service. It enables subscribers to browse or search for songs, artists, or genres in Spotify's collection and to select which songs they wish to hear. Subscribers may also select a genre and listen to a "radio station" composed of songs, selected by Spotify, in that genre. "Premium" subscribers (those with paid subscriptions) may also download music to listen offline.

To provide its music streaming and download services, Spotify must both bargain for various voluntary copyright licenses and comply with requirements for compulsory licenses.

Recall that under the Copyright Act, a music recording consists of two distinct copyrightable works. The first is the musical work—created by a composer and perhaps written down in music notation. The second is the sound engineer's recording of a particular performance of that musical work in the studio or on stage. (A third component is the recording artists' right in the live music performance, but I will put that aside here.) Those two works—the music composition and the sound recording of a particular performance—are embodied together in the music recording that we listen to online. But each has its own separate copyright. As a result, Spotify cannot stream or provide digital downloads of recorded music unless it has cleared all necessary rights for both the music compositions and the sound recordings.

Further, different entities likely own the applicable rights in each work. The copyright in the musical composition is owned initially by the songwriter but is often assigned to a music publisher, such as Universal Music Publishing Group, which specializes in marketing and licensing music. In turn, music publishers typically divide up the authority to negotiate and grant different types of rights to use their music. As we have seen, ASCAP and BMI represent the vast majority of American songwriters and music publishers in granting licenses to publicly perform music, including to stream music over the Internet. A different body, the Harry Fox Agency, represents the majority of American songwriters and music publishers in granting "mechanical" licenses. Mechanical licenses are licenses to make and distribute phonorecords embodying musical works. (Recall that the Copyright Act defines "phonorecords" as "material objects in which sounds, other than those accompanying a motion picture or other audiovisual work, are fixed . . . and from which the sounds can be perceived, reproduced, or otherwise communicated.") A mechanical license is also required to sell digital downloads of musical compositions, and, arguably, to make buffer copies in the course of online streaming.

Not only do different collective rights management organizations grant and administer licenses for different rights, but those licenses are also governed by very different sets of legal rules. As discussed above, ASCAP and BMI typically grant blanket licenses for all songs in their respective repertoires, and those licenses are subject to the constraints of antitrust consent decrees under the continuing supervision of an antitrust rate court. By contrast, the Harry Fox Agency and independent music publishers grant mechanical licenses under the shadow of Section 115 of the Copyright Act. Section 115 provides for a statutory license, with rates determined by the Copyright Royalty Board on a per song basis, although the Board applies a percentage of revenue formula for interactive streaming. Each regime imposes its own idiosyncratic mechanisms for obtaining licenses and for determining and paying royalties.

And that is just the musical composition. Recall that Spotify must also clear the rights to stream and sell downloads of sound recordings—sound engineers' recordings of particular performances of musical compositions. The copyright in the sound recording is typically owned by the record label. Spotify will have to negotiate with each record label for a license to distribute downloads of the label's sound recordings and to stream recordings that are chosen by Spotify users. On the other hand, for Spotify's online radio station (or "webcasting") service, Spotify can enjoy the benefits of a statutory license for webcasters under the Copyright Act. Under the statutory license provisions, webcasters pay the statutory license fees to Sound Exchange, a collective rights management organization that collects those fees on the behalf of record labels.

Finally, if that licensing morass were not bad enough, today's music industry lacks a single definitive mapping between music recordings and the music compositions they embody. Spotify obtains its music recordings from record labels, and record labels do not keep track of all the musical works embodied in their recordings. And while music publishers follow international standards for identifying songs by title and composer, that data is often gathered after a recording is released, meaning that it does not appear in those music recordings' digital metadata. In short, there is no comprehensive, up-to-date database identifying who owns the copyright in the music compositions embodied in recorded music. Rather, each music industry player keeps its own incomplete records. As a result, Spotify has no practical way of identifying all the musical works it is streaming or offering to its premium subscribers for download.

That's not an issue for Spotify's public performance licenses. Performance rights organizations like ASCAP and BMI typically provide a blanket license for all music in their respective repertoires. But the compulsory mechanical license for providing downloads of music compositions requires per song payment. Moreover, the Copyright Royalty Board has ruled that even online streaming entails the making of various phonorecords, including buffer copies, that require a mechanical license. The Copyright Act provides a temporary work-around to this problem. It permits those who distribute recorded music to set aside mechanical license fees until the distributor can identify the rights holders. Nonetheless, without admitting fault, Spotify has paid tens of millions of dollars to settle music publisher claims that it failed to pay required mechanical royalties.[6]

One such settlement purportedly calls for Spotify to invite record labels, music publishers, performance rights organizations, and competing online music services to establish a "Copyright Data Sharing Committee" to confidentially discuss sharing music catalog data in order to make mechanical licensing easier and more accurate. It remains to be seen whether anything will come of that initiative to bring together the music industry's notoriously fractious players to share their proprietary data.

Online music services like Spotify must offer complete catalogues of recorded music to be commercially viable. That requires obtaining licenses for millions of songs and sound recordings—a time-consuming, expensive, and burdensome task. It reportedly took Spotify two years to obtain all the licenses it needed to launch its service—and even then, Spotify got hit with music publisher lawsuits for failing to identify all the music compositions included in its service.

Moreover, Spotify is not alone. Music streaming services Rhapsody, Tidal, Slacker, Google Play, and Apple Music have also been sued by independent songwriters for allegedly failing to set aside mechanical license fees for all songwriters.

The Copyright Office issued a report in February 2015 presenting legislative proposals that, according to the report, would simplify music licensing and provide more licensing revenue to songwriters and music publishers.[7] Among other policy recommendations, the Copyright Office proposed that music publishers should be entitled to opt out of ASCAP and BMI to negotiate individual licenses for interactive streaming services (which enable the consumer to choose which song to hear). That proposal makes little sense to this observer. Facilitating copyright holder exit from collective licensing would hardly simplify music licensing. More helpfully, however, the Copyright Office also proposed changes in the law to enable collective rights management organizations to license both performance and mechanical rights, rather than divvying up those rights between performance licensing organizations (ASCAP and BMI) and mechanical rights organizations (Harry Fox).

As of this writing, Congress has yet to take action on any of the Copyright Office's music licensing recommendations. However, several members of Congress have recently introduced proposed legislation, titled the Music Modernization Act, which would establish a new collective management organization with authority to grant blanket licenses for all musical works to music download and streaming services.

Exceptions and Limitations to Copyright Owner Rights

What are exceptions and limitations to copyright owner rights?

Copyrights are exclusive, proprietary rights. As a general rule, no one may copy or otherwise use a copyrighted work in a way that falls within one of the exclusive rights unless and until the copyright owner gives permission. But that is not always the case. Copyright law recognizes a number of instances in which the copyright owner's permission is not required to use a work in a way that would otherwise infringe the copyright.

In copyright law parlance, a copyright "exception" means that the user may use the work without the copyright owner's permission and without having to pay the copyright owner for using the work. Fair use is the primary copyright exception under the U.S. Copyright Act. A copyright "limitation" typically means that the user may use the work without the copyright owner's permission but does need to pay a license fee for that privilege in an amount established by a tribunal of copyright royalty judges in accordance with a formula set out in the Copyright Act. A copyright "limitation" might also refer to limits that the Copyright Act imposes on all copyrights, such as copyright's limited term.

What is fair use?

Fair use is a defense to copyright infringement. If you copy, perform, display, or build upon a work in a manner that qualifies as fair use, you have not infringed the copyright and you do not need the copyright owner's permission.

Fair use is a judicially created doctrine, stemming back to the nineteenth century. Congress codified fair use in the Copyright Act of 1976. The Act sets out four factors for courts to consider on a case-by-case basis to determine whether what would otherwise be an infringing use is excused as a fair use. These include: (1) the purpose of the defendant's use; (2) the nature of the copyrighted work (fiction or factual, published or unpublished); (3) the amount the defendant copied; and (4) the effect of the use on the potential market for the copyrighted work. Courts may consider other factors as well.

As the courts currently interpret and apply fair use, a key for determining fair use is whether the defendant's use is "transformative"—although nontransformative uses can also be fair use. If the court finds that the allegedly infringing use is transformative, it will almost always find that the use is a fair use, unless the defendant copied more than reasonably necessary for the use. A use is transformative if the defendant used the copyrighted work for a different expressive purpose from that for which the copyrighted work was originally created or if the defendant used the copyrighted work merely as raw material for substantially new expression that conveys a different message or artistic conception from the copyrighted work.

To copy from a copyrighted work in order to parody it is a classic transformative use. But there are many other types of uses that regularly qualify as transformative as well.

For example, a court held that Google's mass digitization of books to create a searchable database of their text is a "highly transformative" use of those literary works. Central to the court's ruling was that, although Google makes digital copies of entire books in order to create a comprehensive database, it displays to users only a couple sentences of books that remains in copyright, just enough to show the context in which the user's search term appears in the book. As the court put it: "Google Books digitizes books and transforms expressive text into a comprehensive word index that helps readers, scholars, researchers, and others find books. The use of book text to facilitate search through the display of snippets is transformative. . . . Google Books does not supersede or supplant books because it is not a tool to be used to read books. Instead it 'adds value to the original' and allows for 'the creation of new information, new aesthetics, new insights and understandings.' "[8]

Likewise, a court held that a book publisher's incorporation of thumbnail reproductions of concert posters in an illustrated history of the Grateful Dead was a transformative use of the original artistic images that appeared on the posters. The court reasoned that the original images had been created for the dual purpose of artistic expression and concert promotion. In contrast, the reproductions in the defendant's book served a different expressive purpose: historic artifacts that enhance the understanding of the biographical text.

We will return to fair use in greater detail in Chapter IV below.

What are statutory or compulsory licenses?

As we have seen, copyright owners enjoy a bundle of exclusive rights to use authors' works. If you wish to reproduce, publicly perform, publicly display, or otherwise use a work in a manner that falls within one or more of those exclusive rights, you must first obtain the copyright owner's permission to do so. You must, in other words, come to some agreement with the copyright owner over the amount of payment and terms of use.

However, the Copyright Act also provides for a number of so-called statutory or compulsory licenses for various types of uses, ranging from making cover recordings of popular songs to cable operators' retransmissions of over-the-air television broadcasts. If a use is covered by a statutory license, the user must pay a license fee at a rate that is determined by a panel of three Copyright Royalty Judges (a body of administrative judges appointed by the Librarian of Congress), in accordance with the applicable standard for determining the rate set out in the Copyright Act. If the user qualifies for a statutory license, the user need not obtain the copyright owner's permission for the use. From the copyright owner's perspective, the license is thus compulsory; the copyright owner has no right to prevent the use so long as the user pays the administratively determined license fee.

Historically, Congress has enacted compulsory licenses to enable new technological media to take root, free from the threat that incumbent copyright industries will use their exclusive rights to stifle a perceived threat to their dominance and business model. Media that have benefitted from compulsory licenses have included the then-nascent sound recording industry (in the early twentieth century), cable television, satellite broadcasts, Internet radio (or "webcasters"), public broadcasters, and jukeboxes. Typically, new technological media initially contend that copyright law does not apply to their activity, while the copyright industries press the claim that the new media's dissemination of copyrighted works will destroy the incentive to create new works. Congress then steps in to work out a compromise under which the new media may continue to disseminate without the copyright owner's permission, but the copyright owners receive compensation pursuant to a statutory license.

The Copyright Act provides that the Copyright Royalty Judges must set a compulsory license rate "to afford the copyright owner a fair return for his or her creative work and the copyright user a fair income under existing economic conditions."[9] Under that "fair return/fair income" standard, the Royalty Judges must take into account "the relative roles of the copyright owner and the copyright user in the product made available to the public with respect to relative creative contribution, technological contribution, capital investment, cost, risk, and contribution to the opening of new markets for creative expression and media for their communication."

However, the most recent statutory license, which was enacted for webcasters' digital transmission of sound recordings, sets out a more copyright-owner-favorable "willing seller/willing buyer" standard. That standard is designed to mimic the license rate that the copyright owner would be able to achieve in market negotiations. In applying the willing seller/willing buyer standard, therefore, Royalty Judges must determine what would be the licensing rate if copyright owners could refuse to license the use, regardless of the contributions the user brings to the table.

The Copyright Office has taken the position that the willing seller/willing buyer standard should apply to all music licensing. In contrast, webcasters, such as Pandora, have argued that the compulsory license rate set in accordance with the willing seller/willing buyer standard is unfairly onerous and threatens to drive them out of business. As the webcasters point out, under the Copyright Act, satellite radio operates under the older fair return/fair income standard, and terrestrial radio pays no royalties at all for broadcasting sound recordings. Pandora lobbied Congress to enact the "Internet Radio Fairness Act," which would apply a fair return/fair income standard to determine the compulsory license rate for webcasting. So far, Congress has not acceded to Pandora's requested relief. Nor has Congress enacted recording-industry-sponsored legislation that would require terrestrial radio stations to obtain permission from record labels to broadcast sound recordings.

A variant of the statutory licenses is the private copying levy established under the Audio Home Recording Act of 1992. Under that Copyright Act amendment, consumers are entitled to make noncommercial private copies of recorded music using equipment that is designed for copying music (but not personal computers). In return, manufacturers of digital musical recording devices and media must pay a levy on each device and recording media, with the levy proceeds distributed to the rights holders.

The Audio Home Recording Act is of little direct effect today since consumers typically use personal computers, not dedicated digital music recording devices (such as digital cassette players), to copy recorded music. Outside the United States, however, copyright laws commonly provide for private copying exceptions for a broad range of private copying, generally coupled with levies on copying equipment and media. A number of commentators (including this author) have proposed enacting some form of the private copying levy model in the United States, including imposing levies on Internet service providers, personal computers, and mobile devices in return for exempting noncommercial file sharing from any claim for copyright infringement.

Does the First Amendment right to free speech impose limits on copyright?

The First Amendment provides that Congress shall make no law that abridges freedom of speech. At first glance, copyright law seems to run afoul of that prohibition. After all, freedom of speech is not limited to words that we create. The First Amendment also protects our right to stand on a street corner and hand out copies of *The Communist Manifesto*, the *Koran*, or another writing that was authored by someone else. But copyright law abridges that freedom. Because of copyright law, I may be prevented from distributing a copyrighted writing authored by someone else even if I wish to do so to convey my own political or artistic message. I may also be prevented from modifying someone else's copyrighted expression in order to convey my message.

So how can copyright law comport with the First Amendment? Can it be that copyright law is unconstitutional?

The basic answer is that, as interpreted by the courts, the First Amendment prohibition on abridging freedom of speech is not absolute. Courts rather apply a variety of tests to determine when laws and regulations that burden speech nonetheless pass First Amendment muster. In the case of copyright, the Supreme Court has held that copyright law does not conflict with the First Amendment because it accommodates free speech in two ways. The first is the idea/expression dichotomy discussed above. A copyright holder may not prevent the speaker from copying ideas, facts, or information found in a copyrighted work. Rather copyright law prevents the speaker only from copying the literal form in which the copyright holder has expressed them. The second is fair use. There are times in which copying or building upon copyrighted expression, not just facts or ideas, is central to conveying one's message. According to the Supreme Court, fair use enables speakers to copy and build upon existing works when necessary to convey a different, new message.

In so holding, the Supreme Court has applied to copyright law a First Amendment test known as "definitional balancing." So long as copyright law contains the idea/expression dichotomy and fair use privilege, it complies with First Amendment strictures. But, the Supreme Court has suggested, if either of those vital free speech safeguards were to be eliminated or substantially weakened, whether by Congress or the courts, copyright law would impermissibly burden freedom of speech.

More Key Terms and Concepts

What is the public domain?

Authors' works inevitably go into the public domain when their copyright term has expired. If an author's work is in the public domain, it is not subject to any copyright protection. Public domain works may be freely copied, distributed, modified, and incorporated into new works.

If I add new creative expression to a public domain work, I have a copyright in the new, creative elements of my work (but not in the public domain elements), so long as my new contributions are sufficiently creative and substantial. Hence, anyone is free to make his or her own motion picture version of Shakespeare's *Romeo and Juliet*, which is in the public domain. But no one may copy the original cinematography, scenery, music, and direction from previous copyright-protected motion picture adaptations of *Romeo and Juliet*.

The expiration of the copyright term is not the only way a work can enter the public domain. A work can also be in the public domain because its copyright owner has forfeited his or her copyright. That might occur if the copyright owner published the work without the requisite copyright notice prior to March 1, 1989 (when the notice requirement for new works was abolished). The Copyright Act also provides that works created by U.S. government employees within the scope of their employment are not protected by copyright. Such works, similarly, might be said to be in the public domain. Works created and first published in a country with which the United States does not have copyright relations, such as Iran, are also in the public domain in the United States.

A work can also enter the public domain if the copyright owner abandons the copyright or dedicates the work to the public domain. To be effective, abandonment must be manifested by some overt act indicating an intention to abandon the copyright.

Commentators' appreciation of the public domain depends largely on their view of copyright. Those who favor a short-term, narrow copyright celebrate the public domain as a fount of knowledge, cultural heritage, and raw material for new creativity. In their view, copyright law serves principally to enrich the public domain by spurring the creation of new works that enjoy copyright protection only for a limited time—the more limited, the better. By contrast, copyright industry spokepersons argue that a long or even perpetual copyright would enhance public access by providing incentives for publishers and studios to maintain and disseminate old works. As Jack Valenti, former president of the Motion Picture Association of America (MPAA), colorfully put it: "A public domain work is an orphan. No one is responsible for its life . . . [and] it becomes soiled and haggard."

Empirical studies do not support Valenti's dismissive view of the public domain. Publishers regularly issue new editions and releases of public domain works. Indeed, a comparison of public domain works from the 1910s and early 1920s with their still copyrighted counterparts from the later 1920s reveals that today's publishers distribute to the public many more of the public domain works than the comparable in-copyright works.[10] Further, copyrights in out-of-print works have proven to be a significant obstacle to mass digitization projects, which aim to make large numbers of digital copies of predigital works freely available online. It can be prohibitively costly to determine who owns the relevant copyrights in such works, let alone to negotiate with each of millions of copyright owners for inclusion of their works in a publicly available online database.

What is a derivative work?

One of the copyright owner's exclusive rights is the right "to prepare derivative works based upon the copyrighted work."

A derivative work is broadly defined as any form in which the underlying copyrighted work "may be recast, transformed, or adapted." It includes translations, musical arrangements, dramatizations, fictionalizations, motion picture versions, sound recordings, art reproductions, abridgments, condensations, remixes, and edited versions.

Recall that courts have broadly construed the right to copy as encompassing the right to make nonliteral copies, not just exact copies of all or part of the copyrighted work. As a result, the right to prepare derivative works largely overlaps the right to copy. Under today's copyright law, most unauthorized translations, motion picture adaptations, abridgements, and remixes would infringe the right to make (nonliteral) copies and would thus infringe copyright even if there were no derivative right.

Nonetheless, some copyright critics have expressed concern that the derivative right unduly burdens creative adaptations of existing works. Some advocate eliminating the derivative right. Others argue that the derivative right should be a right only to equitable remuneration, not an exclusive right. In that view, the derivative creator should have to pay the copyright owner a license fee that depends on the relative value of the underlying work versus the derivative creator's own creative contribution, but should not have to obtain the copyright owner's permission to create the derivative work. Copyright industry supporters retort that the exclusive right to prepare derivative works is a vital part of the copyright incentive and stands at the heart of established licensing practices within those industries. For example, movie studios acquire motion picture rights in novels on the assumption that they then have the exclusive right to make a movie based on the novel.

What are an author's moral rights?

The term "moral right" is a translation from the French *droit moral*. Despite the reference to "moral," moral rights refer not to ethical norms, but to the legal right of authors to control the timing and manner in which their works are disseminated to the public. Moral rights consist, most importantly, of the rights of integrity and attribution. The moral right of integrity consists of the author's right to prevent unwanted distortions and presentations of a work that might harm the author's reputation or run contrary to the author's artistic conception. The moral right of attribution gives authors the right to insist upon authorship credit, whether under the author's true name or the author's chosen pseudonym.

Moral rights are primarily personal rights, like an individual's right to prevent defamatory harm to her reputation and invasion of her privacy. As such, moral rights stand independent from authors' exclusive right of economic exploitation of their works under copyright law. Indeed, moral rights can be enforced even against a publisher or studio that holds the copyright in a work. For example, the French Supreme Court held that the heirs of film director John Huston could assert Huston's moral right of integrity to prevent the broadcast of a colorized version of Huston's film noire classic, *Asphalt Jungle*, on French television even though the French broadcaster held a copyright license from Ted Turner, the film's copyright owner.

The Berne Convention for the Protection of Literary and Artistic Works, to which the United States acceded in 1989, provides that countries who are parties to that treaty must accord the moral rights of integrity and attribution to authors who are nationals of other Berne Convention countries. However, leading copyright stakeholders in the United States have long viewed moral rights as antithetical to the system of economic incentives and transferable literary property that is said to undergird U.S. copyright law. Consequently, when the United States acceded to the Berne Convention, Congress expressly declined to enact a moral rights amendment to the Copyright Act. Rather Congress found that a combination of rights under various laws provide a colorable approximation of the moral rights that the Berne Convention requires. These include copyright (so long as the author still owns the copyright), unfair competition, defamation, and privacy law.

Since then, U.S. courts, led by the Supreme Court's 2003 ruling in *Dastar Corp. v. Twentieth Century Fox*, have largely gutted authors' use of unfair competition law to prevent distortions to their work and to require authorship credit. As a result, it is highly questionable today whether the United States complies with the moral rights requirements of the Berne Convention.

In 1990, Congress enacted the Visual Artists Rights Act (VARA), which provides for a very limited version of moral rights for creators of fine art. VARA gives such artists the right to insist upon authorship credit. It also gives artists the right to prevent the intentional distortion, mutilation, or other modification of original or limited edition copies of works of fine art that would be prejudicial to the artist's reputation. Artists may also disavow authorship in the event such a modification is nonintentional. In addition, creators of works of "recognized stature" may prevent the intentional or grossly negligent destruction of their work.

In contrast to most moral rights laws outside the United States, VARA does not give artists the right to prevent someone from making and then modifying a *copy* of the artist's work. If Leonardo da Vinci were a contemporary American artist, he could rely on VARA to prevent someone from physically painting a mustache on his original canvas of the *Mona Lisa*. But VARA would give him no right to prevent someone from photoshopping a mustache onto a digital reproduction of the *Mona Lisa* and then posting that mustached *Mona Lisa* on the web. Nor does VARA provide any moral rights to artists in works-made-for hire or to novelists, filmmakers, or any other authors aside from creators of fine art.

The question whether U.S. copyright law should contain a broader recognition of moral rights has been the subject of some debate, including in congressional hearings regarding the colorization of black-and-white films in the late 1980s.

There have also been a couple of widely publicized copyright infringement lawsuits in which songwriters have objected to the use of their songs in commercials or to support political candidates whom the songwriter found objectionable. Those might be thought of as efforts to use copyright law to vindicate a moral right of integrity. However, moral rights have not generally been the focus of battles over copyright in the digital arena. If anything, there seems to be widespread consensus among users of social media that those who remix or repost someone else's creation should credit the original author—and those who fail to do so are widely criticized.

As of this writing, the Copyright Office is conducting a public study "to assess the current state of U.S. law recognizing and protecting moral rights for authors, specifically the rights of attribution and integrity."[11] The Office has asked for public comment as part of this study to determine whether it should recommend moral rights legislation.

Notably, the Copyright Office moral rights inquiry has brought together some strange bedfellows. Copyright industry trade associations (including the Motion Picture Association of America, Recording Industry Association of America, and Association of American Publishers) have joined with frequent copyright skeptics (such as the American Library Association, Association of Research Libraries, Electronic Frontier Foundation, and Public Knowledge) in opposing statutory recognition of moral rights in the United States. The copyright industries express concern that moral rights would upset longstanding contractual arrangements, lead to uncertainty in marketing and copyright licensing, and impose restraints on copyright transfers. The copyright skeptics fear that moral rights would impose unacceptable burdens on free speech and fair use. By contrast, authors' associations, not surprisingly, support statutory recognition of moral rights. It remains to be seen whether the Copyright Office will propose that Congress enact moral rights legislation.

What are orphan works?

Recall that copyrights remain in force for a very long time, often upward of a century. In addition, copyright arises automatically when the author fixes the work in a tangible means of expression. Copyright protection does not require registration, a copyright notice, or renewal. Nor do copyright transfers have to be recorded.

Copyrights' long duration and the absence of mandatory registration, notice, renewal, or recording transfers have given rise to a widespread phenomenon known as "orphan works." For some works, the author has long ago died, the author's heirs are unknown, and the publisher has gone out of business, with no record of copyright transfers. As a result, even though the work might still be in copyright, no one knows who owns the copyright or how to locate the copyright owner. In addition, millions of works are created and posted on the Internet (or distributed offline) without identifying the author or indicating how the author can be located.

Such works are said to be orphaned. It is not possible to obtain a copyright license to use an orphan work. As a result, no one can build on orphan works, incorporate them into new works, or make them available to the public without risking that a putative copyright owner will appear out of the woodwork and sue for infringement.

The orphan works problem is widespread. One comprehensive study concluded that of approximately 2 million books published in the United States since 1920, some 600,000 should be considered orphans. And that does not include artworks, photographs, pamphlets, and other types of work for which the copyright owner cannot be identified or located.

The Copyright Office issued a report on orphan works in 2006. It has also supported legislation that, in the Office's view, would ease the orphan works problem. The proposed legislation would limit the exposure to copyright infringement liability of any user who has undertaken a good faith diligent search for the copyright holder and completed certain notice and authorship attribution requirements.

Some critics of that proposed legislation argue that it does not go far enough to immunize users of orphan works from potential copyright infringement liability. As a result, even if Congress were to enact the proposed legislation, millions of orphan works would effectively remain unusable. From the opposite side, author organizations like the American Society of Media Photographers argue that the proposed legislation would wrongfully deny copyright protection for some authors by absolving users of having to obtain a copyright license in advance of use. As of yet, Congress has not enacted any orphan works legislation.

Going forward, digital technology presents a partial solution to the orphan works problem. Authors can embed copyright ownership and licensing information in digital copies of their works. The Copyright Act already prohibits the intentional removal or alteration of any such "copyright management information" without the copyright owner's permission. Some observers also favor the establishment of voluntary online copyright registries to help trace copyright owners. But absent a rule that requires copyright owners to provide current, updated information regarding copyright transfers on an ongoing basis, many works will remain orphaned.

What are statutory damages?

The Copyright Act gives copyright owners a choice of monetary remedy for copyright infringement. A successful copyright infringement plaintiff may elect to recover either: (1) actual damages caused by infringement plus the infringer's profits from infringement that are not already taken into account in computing damages; or (2) an award of statutory damages for each work that has been infringed. As set forth in the Copyright Act, statutory damages may total up to $30,000 per work if the infringement was not committed willfully and up to $150,000 per work for willful infringement.

Statutory damages are available only if the infringed work was registered with the Copyright Office prior to the infringement. Congress intended statutory damages to serve a dual purpose. First, copyright owners who elect statutory damages need not submit proof of actual harm caused by the infringement. This is especially useful for copyright owners when the infringed work is unpublished or has a small market. Second, the option of statutory damages serves as a deterrent to copyright infringement. As one court noted: "Congress intended the statutory damages to be 'substantially' higher than actual damages. . . . 'It is important that the cost of infringement substantially exceed the costs of compliance, so that persons who use or distribute intellectual property have a strong incentive to abide by the copyright laws."[12] In other words, statutory damages further the policies behind punitive damages.

Statutory damages have come to be immensely controversial as applied to cases involving copyright infringements of multiple works over the Internet. Since statutory damages are calculated per work that has been infringed and may be awarded even absent proof of any actual harm, social media sites and other user-generated content platforms risk statutory damages liability in the many millions of dollars if held liable for infringement of multiple works. Viacom's billion-dollar claim against YouTube is a prime example. Viacom alleged that YouTube should be required to pay statutory damages for each of hundreds of thousands of infringing videos that YouTube subscribers had uploaded onto the platform. YouTube and Viacom ultimately settled, with no finding of any infringement liability on YouTube's part. But MP3.com, a site that enabled users to listen to the songs residing in their CD collection over the Internet, was not so lucky. MP3.com went bankrupt after a court announced that the company would be subject to a statutory damages award of up to $118 million, based on the court's finding that MP3.com had infringed up to 4,700 songs. Statutory damages have also been the basis for sizable awards against individual peer-to-peer file sharers. In one much-discussed case, a jury awarded statutory damages of $675,000 against file sharer Joel Tenenbaum.

Critics of such awards argue that Congress should amend the Copyright Act to require that statutory damages more closely correspond with actual harm. Defenders counter that Congress raised the statutory damage ceiling to the current $150,000 per each work that the infringer has willfully infringed primarily to deter massive infringements over the Internet. Indeed, the legislation providing for the increase was titled the Digital Theft Deterrence and Copyright Damages Improvement Act of 1999.

What is the Internet service provider safe harbor?

Copyright law provides for "secondary liability" for copyright infringement. Under certain circumstances, if you make it possible for someone else to infringe a copyright or if you profit from someone else's copyright infringement when you have the right to supervise that person's conduct, you are liable for that person's infringement even though you did not make any infringing copies yourself. Under traditional principles of secondary liability, Internet intermediaries—including user-generated content sites, social media sites, and Internet access providers—risk liability for their users' copyright infringements. That was the basis of Viacom's billion-dollar lawsuit against YouTube. Likewise, search engines could face liability for facilitating access to infringing websites.

Internet intermediaries insist that they have no ready way to prevent such infringements. Certainly, they would be hard-pressed to vet the millions of files that users post—or the millions of websites that appear in response to user search queries—every day. If Internet service providers were required to undertake that costly effort in order to avoid liability, far fewer companies would be willing to invest in providing and improving the Internet services upon which we have come to depend.

To avoid that prospect, Congress enacted a safe harbor from liability for Internet service providers. The safe harbor was part of the Digital Millennium Copyright Act (DMCA) of 1998. So long as an Internet service provider meets the requirements of the safe harbor, it will not be liable for infringements that take place through its service.

The safe harbor requirements are complex and vary somewhat depending on which type of Internet service is provided. But basically—as confirmed by the courts—the safe harbor puts the primary burden of policing the Internet for copyright infringements on copyright holders, not Internet service providers. Accordingly, Internet service providers need not actively police for infringement or implement costly filtering systems to block infringing activity. Nor are Internet service providers liable just because they know as well as anyone that their users post a lot of infringing material on their system. Rather, Internet service providers will typically enjoy the safe harbor so long as they: (1) do not knowingly facilitate or turn a blind eye to specific identified infringements on their system; (2) expeditiously take down infringing material specifically identified in "takedown notices" submitted by copyright holders (further explained in the next question); and (3) have a reasonable policy of terminating service to users who repeatedly infringe copyright. Further, as courts have construed the safe harbor provisions, service providers are under no obligation to remove infringing material identified in a copyright holder's takedown notice unless the notice provides the specific web address where the material is located. The service provider need not search for or remove other infringing copies of the same work unless the copyright holder identifies the web addresses where they are located as well.

The Internet service provider safe harbor was part of a grand bargain between the copyright and telecommunications industries that found expression in the DMCA. The DMCA enhances copyright owners' ability to protect their copyrighted works from infringement online. It does so primarily by prohibiting the circumvention of "digital rights management"—encryption that copyright owners use to control access to their works, such as the software code that prevents anyone other than subscribers from accessing pay content on Hulu or Netflix. In return, the DMCA imposes the primary duty to police for online infringement on copyright owners, not Internet intermediaries.

Nonetheless, copyright industries now lobby Congress to impose greater policing and filtering requirements on Internet intermediaries. They point to the emergence and explosive growth of peer-to-peer file trading, social media, BitTorrent, and pirate streaming sites since Congress enacted the DMCA in 1998. They argue that courts have construed the DMCA safe harbor provisions far too favorably for Internet service providers and that massive online copyright infringement cannot be curbed without imposing significant policing responsibilities on social media, search engines, and other Internet intermediaries.

Copyright industries also contend that courts have too broadly interpreted which types of online services are potentially eligible for the safe harbor. As courts have interpreted the statutory language, the DMCA safe harbor for hosting infringing material stored by users does not merely immunize online services that facilitate user storage without any other service provider involvement. Courts have also construed the safe harbor to immunize Internet service providers that are actively involved in making user-posted content accessible to the public. As interpreted by courts, for example, YouTube and Vimeo fall within the safe harbor for services that store material at the direction of the user even though those platforms do not merely host user-posted videos, but also format, index, stream, and curate them. Copyright industries argue that social media sites with that level of involvement should face liability for their users' infringing postings.

Given the immense scale of online infringements and Internet intermediaries' central role in our communication and information ecosystem, the issue of how, if at all, the safe harbor provisions should be recalibrated has central importance for copyright policy. In that light, the Copyright Office has recently launched a study to evaluate the impact and effectiveness of the safe harbor provisions, including the notice and takedown system, which I discuss next. The Office called for public comment as part of its study and has received tens of thousands of comments from stakeholders, public interest organizations, academics, and interested individuals. I examine the debate over the safe harbor in more detail in Chapter V below.

What is notice and takedown?

Notice and takedown is a procedure by which copyright owners send notices to social media sites, search engines, and other online service providers to inform them of allegedly infringing material that is available on or through the service provider's site. In response, the service provider takes down or removes links to the material. Importantly, the takedown notice must identify the copyrighted work alleged to be infringed, the material that the copyright owner alleges is infringing, and the website address or other such information that the online service provider needs in order to find and remove the allegedly infringing material.

When the takedown notice concerns material that an Internet user has uploaded onto the service provider's platform, the service provider must notify the user of its receipt of the takedown notice. The Internet user may then send the service provider a counter-notice asserting that the material is not infringing. Upon receiving a counter-notice, the service provider may repost the material and let the parties fight out their dispute in court.

The notice and takedown procedure has arisen from provisions of the DMCA establishing the safe harbor from copyright infringement liability for Internet service providers (see the question above). Internet service providers enjoy immunity from liability for their users' copyright infringements if they implement the notice and takedown procedure, expeditiously take down infringing material, and comply with various other requirements.

Notice and takedown takes place on a massive scale. The sheer number of notices and takedowns—and their probable impact on online media and communication—far exceed that of copyright infringement litigation in court. Large copyright holders deploy automated systems, which use software bots to scour the Internet for copyright infringements and then generate and send takedown notices to the applicable Internet service provider. Those automated systems generate a huge volume of takedown notices. For example, Google reports that its search engine receives some one billion takedown notices per year.[13] In turn, Google and other large online service providers have implemented automated takedown systems, using their own computer algorithms, although small service providers still rely entirely on human review of takedown notices.

By contrast, the counter-notice procedure, by which users who post allegedly infringing material can resist takedown, is rarely used. That is not surprising. First, the DMCA does not require a counter-notice procedure when a search engine removes a link to an allegedly infringing website. Thus, the counter-notice procedure is not relevant to the more than one billion takedown notices per year that Google and other search engines receive. The only way website proprietors know that a search engine no longer links to their site is to do a search on the search engine. Second, with respect to user-posted material, for which the counter-notification procedure does apply, a large percentage of targeted material is blatantly infringing. A user who posts blatantly infringing material is unlikely to file a counter-notice objecting to its removal. Finally, even when the copyright holder's claim of infringement is erroneous or questionable (and studies have found that a substantial minority fall within that category), individuals often lack

the copyright knowledge, wherewithal, and willingness to litigate required to send a counter-notice. In that regard, sending a
counter-notice requires that the sender submit to federal court
jurisdiction and agree to have his or her identity divulged to
the copyright owner.

Congress designed the notice and takedown procedure
and online service provider safe harbor to balance two goals.
First, they give copyright holders a relatively inexpensive,
easy mechanism for obtaining removal of infringing material
from the Internet. Second, they give online service providers
the opportunity to invest in providing their services free from
the risk of liability for their users' infringements. However,
the mushrooming of peer-to-peer file trading, social media,
BitTorrent, pirate streaming, and user-generated content sites
have called that balance into question. Copyright holders
complain that notice and takedown provides inadequate protection for them given the massive volume of infringing material online, the requirement that they identify the specific
web address of each infringing copy, and the ease with which
users repost material that has been taken down. By contrast,
service providers and user advocates insist that imposing more
burdensome requirements on online service providers—such
as requiring them to implement expensive proactive filtering
systems—would threaten the continued viability of the online
platforms for user communication, information, and creativity
upon which we have come to enjoy and depend. Moreover,
online civil liberty advocates, such as the Electronic Frontier
Foundation, maintain that automated notice and takedown
systems result in taking down large amounts of material that
does not infringe copyright. They call for greater human review, on the part of both copyright holders and online service
providers, to prevent erroneous and abusive takedowns.

I further discuss the fierce controversy over the Internet
service provider safe harbor and notice and takedown regime
in subsequent chapters.

II

THE BATTLES
OVER COPYRIGHT: OVERVIEW

As we have seen in Chapter I, copyright law reflects a delicate balance. Copyright law provides authors with a set of exclusive rights to copy and disseminate their creative expression. But copyrights are also punctuated by significant exceptions and limitations. These include fair use, the limited duration of copyright protection, and the rule that copyright extends only to the form in which authors express their ideas, not to ideas or facts in and of themselves. Exceptions and limitations to copyright serve to protect the public interest in access to information and creative expression. They also enhance the ability of today's authors to build upon the work of previous generations.

Yet, the rapid emergence of digital technology and social media challenges copyright's delicate balance. It raises numerous questions about whether various online uses of creative expression fall within authors' exclusive rights. It also raises policy questions about how broad authors' exclusive rights should be and about how rigorously copyrights should be enforced against individual users and providers of platforms that users sometimes use to infringe. It is in that whirlwind of uncertainty that heated debates over copyright law and policy arise.

What are the battles over copyright?

Copyright law is fiercely contested. Record labels, movie studios, book publishers, newspapers, and many authors rage that those who share copyrighted music, video, text, and images over the Internet are "stealing" their property. These copyright industries and authors further accuse new media companies—like Google, BuzzFeed, Pinterest, Pandora, Spotify, Facebook, Amazon, Apple, and now-defunct Aereo— of brazenly underwriting massive copyright infringement or grossly underpaying creators for the distribution of creative expression.

Those who advocate for rigorous copyright enforcement often present arguments in starkly moralist terms. For them, it is fundamentally wrong to copy, remix, or stream someone else's creation without that person's permission—even if copyright law might currently allow such conduct under certain circumstances. Labels, studios, and publishers also warn of dire consequences if they cannot use copyrights to recoup their investment in producing music, movies, art, newspapers, and books. Without effective copyright enforcement, they insist, our very culture will be impoverished.

By contrast, an array of copyright skeptics celebrate digital technology's power to make vast reservoirs of the world's knowledge and cultural expression readily and cheaply accessible to anyone with an Internet connection—without having to obtain a copyright license before a work is uploaded and shared. The skeptics generally recognize that authors should receive compensation for their creative work. But they argue that copyright is too often used to prop up dinosaur industries and bygone business models. Further, they insist, draconian copyright enforcement against Internet users and new media threatens civil liberties and access to information.

In the skeptics' view, excessive copyright enforcement would also block consumer-friendly technological innovation that enables us to enjoy our music, TV shows, movies, news stories, and books anytime and anywhere. Copyright industries would like to hold technology companies responsible for their customers' use of a company's products or services to infringe copyrights. If the copyright industries are successful, technology companies would have to radically alter our personal computers, communication networks, search engines, social media sites, and mobile devices to prevent consumers from using them to infringe copyrights.

Finally, the skeptics contend, excessive copyright enforcement runs squarely against what is supposed to be copyright law's overriding purpose: promoting creativity. Too much copyright enforcement stifles creators who wish to build upon existing expression as part of producing new artistic creations. From Shakespeare, to Handel, to Picasso, great artists have always plundered the work of their predecessors. And our unprecedented ability to locate items of interest on the Internet, and then to copy, paste, link, modify, and add commentary to them, has made ours a remix and reposting culture. Anyway, as blogger and open Internet activist Cory Doctorow proclaims, creators are really better off developing new ways to earn a living from their work—Internet savvy business models that do not depend on "complaining about piracy" and "treating your customers like thieves."[1]

Who are the combatants?

Conflicts over contested issues of copyright law and policy often pit traditional media against technology companies and social media—what is loosely labeled "Hollywood versus Silicon Valley." This has certainly been the case with headline-grabbing copyright infringement litigation. For example, movie and cable television giant Viacom sued YouTube for over a billion dollars, claiming that YouTube should be liable for facilitating massive copyright infringement on its user-generated content platform. Similarly, when a technology start-up called Aereo offered a service for making over-the-air television available for viewing on computers and mobile devices, it was sued by a consortium of major broadcasters, including CBS Corporation, Comcast's NBC, Disney's ABC, and 21st Century Fox. Likewise, an association of record labels sued peer-to-peer file-trading platform providers Napster, Grokster, Aimster, Streamcast, and Kazaa. And leading book publishers sued Google over the Google Books Library Project, through which Google and its university library partners digitally scanned and created a searchable database of millions of books.

Hollywood versus Silicon Valley battles regularly carry over from courthouses to the halls of Congress, where stakeholders spar over copyright reform. As noted in the Introduction, the proposed Stop Online Piracy Act pitted copyright industries against a broad coalition of social media and other online aggregators of content and information. Similarly, legislative proposals to remake the ground rules for music licensing pit record labels, composers, and music publishers against music streaming services, such as Pandora, Spotify, and YouTube.

Hollywood has also faced off against Silicon Valley in Copyright Office hearings concerning the Copyright Act's Internet service provider "safe harbor" provisions. As we have seen, courts have interpreted those provisions to give Internet service providers like YouTube broad immunity from liability for their users' copyright infringements. Not surprisingly, Internet search and social media companies argue that the safe harbor provisions are working just fine. By contrast, motion picture studios, record labels, and various authors' associations contend that the provisions are seriously broken.

However, while "Hollywood versus Silicon Valley" aptly encapsulates many of the battles over copyright, that is not always the case. Some litigation and jostling for legislative change pit creators against their own publishers, record labels, and studios. Creators have long complained that they are short-changed by those copyright industries, while the copyright industries insist that they are entitled to a healthy return on their investment in production, marketing, distribution, and financial risk. In addition, traditional media have battled among themselves over their respective rights to distribute creative expression. For example, cable and satellite television operators legally transmit television programming to their subscribers under a complex regime of copyright licenses and government regulations. But television studios and broadcasters have sued Cablevision and Dish Network for providing digital equipment and services that enable subscribers to easily record and view television programming whenever they wish—and to automatically skip over commercials.

Record labels and radio broadcasters have also faced off before Congress. At present, the Copyright Act does not require that radio broadcasters obtain record label permission, or even pay record labels anything, to broadcast music recordings over the air. The labels have longed lobbied Congress to give them the right to insist that broadcasters must obtain label permission to broadcast music recordings.

Furthermore, notwithstanding their continuing battles, Hollywood and Silicon Valley increasingly cooperate on some fronts. In particular, major search engine and social media companies have come to voluntary agreements with copyright industries to block infringing content uploaded by users. Those Silicon Valley companies have agreed to such policing measures even though courts have generally absolved them from liability for failing to prevent copyright infringement.

Notably, although the Viacom-YouTube litigation resulted in an overwhelming victory for YouTube, YouTube has voluntarily implemented a "Content ID" system, whereby copyright owners provide digital metadata to flag user-uploaded videos that include the owners' copyrighted film, TV show, or recorded music. Using Content ID, the copyright owner can opt to block a flagged video from appearing on YouTube, leave the video on the platform for promotional value, or monetize it with advertising. Similarly, Google has introduced a "demotion signal" in its search engine algorithm that automatically demotes search results for websites that copyright holders have repeatedly identified as featuring infringing content.

Critics charge that the computer algorithms that Google and other firms use to combat piracy sweep into their net much user-posted content that is fair use or otherwise not infringing. Nevertheless, we can expect more cooperation between Silicon Valley and Hollywood even while they continue to spar in Congress and the courts. It is costly for major technology companies like Google, Facebook, and Apple to assess infringement claims on a case-by-case basis. At some point, it is more cost effective for them to implement technological measures that effectively automate copyright compliance on a mass scale.

Moreover, Silicon Valley and Hollywood increasingly partner to share advertising revenues from user-posted videos that automated copyright compliance software identifies as potentially infringing. YouTube's Content ID is a good example. More than 95 percent of the time, copyright owners choose to monetize, rather than block, user-uploaded videos that Content ID flags as potentially infringing. YouTube and the copyright owner then share the advertising revenue generated for that content.[2] Facebook offers a similar service through the Audible Magic automated content recognition system and Facebook's own Rights Manager video identification system. There, too, Facebook offers rights holders the option of sharing advertising revenue rather than blocking user-posted infringing content. Thus, while Hollywood and Silicon Valley continue to spar bitterly over whether the law should require Internet platforms to implement filtering, in practice, they have implemented a mutually beneficial partnership for tolerating and sharing advertising revenue from millions of user postings that copy popular movies, TV shows, or recorded music without copyright holder permission.

Finally, the lines between Silicon Valley and Hollywood increasing blur as new digital media begin to produce their own content or take a financial interest in creative work that their users post online. Netflix is no longer merely a DVD lending and streaming service of Hollywood (and foreign) movies and TV shows. It has transformed itself to become a major producer of its own programming as well. According to recent reports, Google, Amazon, and Apple are all poised to follow Netflix in producing their own movies and TV shows. And "Amateur" video creators increasingly sign on to Google's AdSense program to earn advertising revenue generated for videos they post on YouTube—revenue that is shared with Google.

How do individual creators' concerns differ from those that impact entire copyright industries?

It is important to unpack copyright issues involving individual creators from those involving entire industries, although the two overlap.

Many creators feel robbed when someone copies their work without their permission or fails to give them authorship credit. For many creators, copyright law must protect authors' exclusive right to decide whether, when, and in what context their creative expression will appear in the public. Along with that right, copyright law must secure authors' prerogative to demand the price they choose for granting permission to exploit their creative work.

Say I write a song about how we are repeatedly fooled by politicians. I might not want my song performed at a particular candidate's campaign rally or recorded by a white racist punk band. Indeed, I might want to prevent anyone copying or performing even a single line from my song without my permission. Many creators feel deeply that it is their right to prevent such unwanted uses of their creative expression—and that copyright law must protect that right. Many also look to revenue from copyright licensing as a significant source of their livelihood.

By contrast, the Internet has spawned a vibrant remix and sharing culture. Millions of social media users regularly copy and post photographs, songs, articles, poems, and videos that they find online. Often they comment on what they post, and others comment on their comments. Social media is also replete with user remixes of popular movies, TV shows, and recorded music. Users often add their own original dialogue to a news or movie clip, as a way of commenting on it, making a joke, or changing its meaning. Others then add their own expression to that video, creating a multiplicity of online video "memes." Or they take parts of several videos or music recordings and merge them together. With digital technology, the possibilities are endless.

For those immersed in remix culture, participants' copying, sharing, commenting on, and modifying expressive works that they find online are integral to creativity and self-expression. For that matter, as noted above, venerated writers, artists, and musicians have long creatively built upon—and sometimes wholesale copied from—the works of their predecessors. T. S. Eliot famously quipped: "Immature poets imitate; mature poets steal."

The Internet has accentuated the debate between creators who insist that anyone who copies from their creative work without their permission is stealing and those who openly celebrate the use of existing works as raw material for self-expression. Yet that debate between largely irreconcilable worldviews is only a part of the battles over copyright. Much of the fight plays out between industries and trade associations, not individual creators and users per se.

Many creators rely on large studios, record labels, or publishers to reach a mass audience. Indeed, many creators are employees of those industries. Creators in some sectors also transfer rights to collective rights management organizations that come to control and enforce rights in millions of creative works. For example, ASCAP (the American Society of Composers, Authors and Publishers) and BMI (Broadcast Music, Inc.) together represent more than 1.4 million songwriters, composers, and music publishers and license more than 23 million songs to radio stations, online music streaming platforms, and retail establishments.

The sheer size and power of those enterprises adds a vast, complex dimension to the battles over copyright. It is one thing to say that an individual songwriter should have the exclusive right to decide who can copy or play a song that he or she has created. It's quite another to say that collective management organizations controlling rights in almost all the recorded songs composed over the past fifty years should have the exclusive right to determine which radio stations, music streaming platforms, and other media they will license to play the songs in their repertoires and which they will not. That would give the collective management organizations inordinate power over the media upon which we rely for our music. It would also effectively give them a veto over new technologies for disseminating music. Armed with the exclusive right to control the performance of virtually all popular songs, the organizations might decide, for example, to refuse to license online music streaming platforms to avoid cannibalizing the societies' hefty revenues from licensing over-the-air broadcast radio stations. For that reason, the two dominant music performance collective management organizations in the United States—ASCAP and BMI—operate under federal antitrust decrees that require that they grant licenses to all media, without discrimination, at reasonable rates.

The same concern arises with respect to the vast swath of copyrights controlled by major movie and TV studios, record labels, and print publishers. For the most part, Hollywood studios—not individual directors and screenwriters—own the copyrights in movies and TV shows; record labels—not recording artists—own copyrights in music recordings; and publishers—not writers—own copyrights in books and news articles. Granting these industries exclusive rights in the content they control threatens to give them considerable power over what creative expression we can access and what technologies are available to disseminate it. The major industries have also traditionally had considerable power over creators, who rely on the industries to reach mass audiences. For those reasons, as with the collective rights management organizations, imposing limits on the copyright industries' exclusive rights might be warranted in certain contexts.

In short, copyright law and policy must give weight to creators' heartfelt views. For that matter, copyright law aims to provide an economic incentive for authors to create—and perhaps even to earn a living from creating full-time. Yet, much of the copyright debate goes far beyond interests of individual creators. It also embroils entire copyright industries, on one hand, versus new technologies and platforms for the dissemination of creative expression, on the other. The stakes for that debate are high. Copyright law does not just provide rights to individual creators in isolation from the industries, media, and collective rights management organizations that traffic in creative expression. Nor, for that matter, do individuals post, engage, and discuss copyrighted content on social media free from the power of Facebook, YouTube, and other social media platforms to promote content that will enhance their advertising revenue. As copyright law operates across markets, social media, and creative sectors, it shapes our system of free expression, cultural production, and communication.

How has digital technology sparked the battles over copyright?

Digital technology stands at the heart of the battles over copyright. The controversies that digital technology has spawned coalesce around three distinct, if sometimes interrelated fronts: file sharing, copyright policing and enforcement, and the competitive threat of new digital media.

File sharing

Think back to before we had personal computers, mobile devices, and the Internet. In that bygone age, if you wanted to read a bestselling novel, you had to buy or borrow the physical book, printed and distributed by its publisher. If you wanted to listen to your favorite Beatles songs over and over, you would buy a record album produced by the Beatles' label—or wait until your favorite radio station played their songs. You could only watch the latest episode of *Cheers* when NBC broadcast it on the air. If you wanted to see a first-run movie, you had to go to the theater where it was playing.

In short, in the predigital age, the so-called copyright industries—movie and TV studios, record labels, and print publishers—had near complete control over the distribution of creative works that populate our culture. Your only real possibility for reading, listening to, or watching such works was to buy a copyright-industry produced copy or to gain access to the work through a copyright-licensed channel or venue. Granted, analog consumer copying equipment—like photocopy machines, VCRs, and cassette recorders—gave consumers the ability to make copies for themselves. But those copies took effort to make and were typically poor, low-quality substitutes for originals produced by copyright industries.

That all changed with the emergence of personal computers and the Internet. We can now, with ease, make perfect digital copies that are indistinguishable from the original. We can also disseminate those copies—as well as stream music, movies, and TV programs—the world over, with our personal computers or mobile devices. Indeed, it takes just one person to post online a digital copy of a popular song or soon-to-be-released motion picture for that work to be available to millions of Internet users from Melbourne to Reykjavik. Digital technology and the Internet empower individuals to bypass traditional copyright industries on an unprecedented scale.

File sharing takes place through a wide variety of peer-to-peer networks, BitTorrent download and streaming portals, user-posted content sites, social media, and cloud storage cyberlockers. Millions of people regularly share files on those platforms without copyright holder permission. An NBCUniversal-commissioned study found that well over

400 million unique Internet users explicitly sought infringing content on file-sharing networks worldwide during a single month—January 2013.[3] Millions of users of social and new media sites like Pinterest, BuzzFeed, and Facebook also regularly copy and repost news stories, music, videos, and photographs they find online.

Copyright owners decry individuals' massive unlicensed dissemination of copyrighted works as "piracy" and "theft." They also contend that pervasive, global file sharing has deprived copyright industries of billions of dollars of revenues and threatens the industries' continued viability—all while the proprietors of file-sharing platforms and social media sites reap huge advertising revenues.

By contrast, some observers view file sharing as a highly efficient means for achieving a great public benefit: putting the entire corpus of cultural expression at our fingertips, unhindered by the daunting obstacle of having to negotiate a license for all works that remain in copyright. Further, they question whether file sharing significantly harms record label and movie studio revenues, especially now that licensed music and video streaming services have taken off. And even if file sharing does threaten those traditional copyright industries, some observers question whether file sharing really harms creators and creativity, given that the industries have always reaped the lion's share of profits from creators' work. In support, they cite the seemingly boundless flow of new video, music, writing, and art that creators post online notwithstanding massive file sharing. Perhaps some creators even thrive on the greater exposure that file sharing provides. Finally, copyright skeptics insist that using copyright law to target file-sharing sites imposes unacceptable burdens on free speech, privacy, and technological innovation. As such, they argue, copyright law should not be deployed to shut down file sharing—an effort which, in any event, is doomed to fail. If file sharing deprives creators of compensation, they contend, alternative mechanisms for compensating creators must be found.

I further explain licensing obstacles and alternative compensation proposals below.

Copyright policing and enforcement

Internet intermediaries are companies that enable users to communicate with one another, find information online, and store digital copies in the cloud for later viewing or listening. They include Internet access providers, search engines, user-generated content sites, cloud storage providers, social media sites, and peer-to-peer communication platforms. Internet intermediaries provide an array of valuable services. Together, they greatly enhance our capacity to locate, store, organize, create, and share information and cultural expression.

But the intermediaries also serve as gateways to prodigious amounts of infringing material, sometimes by design and sometimes as an inadvertent byproduct of their service. Do you want to find Pirate Bay, the notorious BitTorrent site for illicit copies of movies, music, TV shows, games, software, and "much more"? Just search for "Pirate Bay" on Google and follow the link. Want to listen to popular songs or see clips from hit TV shows for free? You can find huge quantities on YouTube, many posted without copyright holder permission. Want to share smartphone recordings you made at a rock concert? Post them on your Facebook page, or store them in your Dropbox and provide your friends (and their friends) with the password.

Copyright industries insist that Internet intermediaries must bear responsibility for facilitating copyright infringement. After all, the intermediaries profit from the multitude of infringing uses of their services whether or not they actively encourage their users to infringe. In the industries' view, copyright law should require Internet intermediaries to police their networks for copyright infringement, implement filtering technologies that block access to infringing material, and disable links to websites that promote piracy.

Internet intermediaries and their supporters argue, by contrast, that copyright law properly puts the burden of copyright policing and enforcement on copyright owners themselves. For intermediaries to determine which of millions of files posted every day are infringing would be an impossible task. As Cory Doctorow puts it: "A really top-notch cable operator might carry two hundred to five hundred TV channels, each one airing ten to twenty-four hours of programming a day. Assuming your cable operator had two hundred channels, that's a minimum of two thousand hours of video a day. As of March 2014, YouTube was adding that much content every twenty minutes. A cable operator might conceivably be required to ensure that a copyright lawyer has inspected all the video that enters its distribution channel, but if we apply that same requirement to YouTube, we would end up exhausting the entire lifespan of every copyright lawyer who ever lived and still not make a dent."[4]

In this view, if Internet intermediaries face potential liability for failing to prevent their users from infringing copyrights, many would simply have to shut down. Moreover, intermediaries that face liability would over-police. Rather than risk liability, search engines would cut links not just to Pirate Bay, but also to websites that feature much noninfringing as well as infringing material. And social media sites would remove any content that copyright holders identify as infringing rather than undergo a costly examination to assess whether that content actually qualifies as noninfringing fair use.

As we have seen, in 1998, Congress stepped in to fashion a "safe harbor" regime under which Internet intermediaries can qualify for immunity from liability for their users' copyright infringements. Under that regime, copyright holders may send intermediaries "takedown" notices that identify infringing material on the intermediaries' system. With some narrow exceptions, so long as the intermediary then expeditiously takes down the infringing content or, for search engines, removes links to infringing websites, the intermediary will enjoy immunity from copyright liability.

Recall that the notice-and-takedown regime swamps judicial copyright law enforcement in the sheer quantity of content involved. Large copyright holders and their enforcement agents use software bots to scour the Internet for content that appears to infringe. The software then sends automated notices of infringement to Internet intermediaries. Large Internet intermediaries, in turn, use automated systems to remove content in response to copyright holder takedown notices. The numbers of notices sent and the amount of content taken down are staggering. Takedown notices sent just to Google Web Search number in the millions each week.

The notice-and-takedown regime has further fueled copyright debates. Copyright industries complain that infringing content is often reposted soon after it is taken down and that Internet intermediaries face no liability for enabling this whack-a-mole phenomenon. At a minimum, they insist, Internet intermediaries should be required not only to take down infringing content, but also to make sure that it stays down. At the same time, a recent study shows that well over a third of automated takedown requests sent to Google Web Search were fundamentally flawed or raised serious questions about their validity. Accordingly, the notice and takedown regime may result in the removal of a considerable amount of noninfringing expression, with no effective judicial oversight.[5]

New digital media

In the heat of debating copyright policy, a crucially important fact is often forgotten: Digital technology would severely disrupt traditional copyright industries even if there were no piracy. The major book publishers, record labels, TV networks, and motion picture studios are "vertically integrated firms"— firms that supply goods and services up and down the supply chain in a particular industry sector. In the analog age, traditional media did not merely *produce* creative works. They also controlled the financing, marketing, and distribution of creative works. Consequently, authors or independent producers who wanted their works disseminated to the public had to contract with a major media firm to do so. In the process, they had to sign away much or all of their copyrights in the work. As such, the major media firms earned far more from their lock on the market for promotion and distribution than from their role in producing creative works.

Record labels, for example, did not merely produce master recordings. Rather, they marshaled vast manufacturing, marketing, and distribution networks to promote radio airplay for their recorded songs and to place record albums on the shelves of retail record stores throughout the country. In that world, only records distributed by major labels could hope to reach a national mass audience.

The labels charged hefty premiums for that vital service. For every sale of an $18 CD, the label received $11 and the retailer $7. From its $11, the label paid music publishers and songwriters a total of about $0.76. In theory, the label also paid a 20-percent royalty to the recording artist. But in 90 percent of the cases, the label deducted the entire royalty from its recording cost, promotional expenses, and other charges, leaving the artist with no cash payment.

Today, however, digital technology is severely undermining record labels' traditional corner on marketing and distribution. Music consumers are increasingly likely to forego record albums and instead buy music through personalized streaming services or digital downloads of individual songs. And we buy our music from new media companies like Pandora, Spotify, Amazon, Google, and Apple. Those companies have their own marketing channels and content curation, as well as the technological capacity to distribute all songs ever recorded.

As a result, traditional record labels now play a substantially diminished role in music marketing and, indeed, no longer offer any advantage in distributing content to consumers. Just the opposite: Technology companies add tremendous value by integrating music content with platforms for search, personalization, social networking, and listening. And unlike the record labels (or brick-and-mortar record stores), music streaming and download services give us the convenience of huge inventories of music instantly available on multiple devices. Apple, Amazon, and Google also support or supply integrated mobile devices for listening to music. In fact, like many new media, these three digital titans are happy to supply music at a low price, as a loss leader for their more profitable goods and services, like iPhones, tablets, and advertising.

In short, new digital media are taking over the market for music distribution because their platforms provide superior and more user-friendly services—and music at a lower price—than have the traditional record labels. The growing dominance of technology companies means that the major record labels can no longer hope to earn their analog-age premium for controlling the distribution of recorded music.

Digital technology also empowers artists to be less dependent on record labels. In the analog era, record labels played a vital role in scouting live music venues for talent, providing high-quality recording studios, financing struggling bands, and mass marketing. In return, record labels garnered the lion's share of revenues for all but the most successful artists; very few artists earned a living from record sales. But digital technology makes it possible to produce high-quality sound and video recordings at a fraction of the cost of analog recording studios. At the same time, record label promotion is also far less crucial than in the predigital era. Social media, user-generated content, and music streaming sites give artists a platform to disseminate their music and build an audience through user recommendations. Quite independently from record label promotion, those sites also offer human and algorithmic curation of content, creating general and personalized recommendations, such as Apple Music's "For You" page. Crowdfunding sites like PledgeMusic and Feed the Muse also offer modest opportunities for musicians to gain seed funding and exposure.

Many aspiring musicians still aim to land a contract with a major label—and labels still offer nontrivial marketing and organizational advantages. Yet digital technology gives musicians unprecedented tools to build a following, and perhaps even earn a living, from a combination of live performances, merchandise sales, user payments for downloads, and streaming service royalties (probably in that order). Major label involvement is no longer critical to musicians' livelihood. An authoritative study of the recording music industry from 1980 to 2010 found that despite a decline in major label releases, the overall number of new recordings brought annually to market since 2000 increased by 50 percent.[6]

In sum, online platforms for streaming and downloading music are a powerful disruptive technology for traditional record labels. Above and beyond piracy, it is this new, digital era competition for music distribution that threatens the demise of traditional record labels as we know them. Artists' reduced dependence on major record labels for talent scouting, production, finance, and marketing also throws the labels' future into doubt.

A similar dynamic applies to other traditional copyright media, including book publishers, newspapers, motion picture studios, music publishers, and TV networks. Digital technology and the emergence of new media distribution platforms have upended the monopoly that those industries once held on distribution and on enabling authors to reach audiences. With the demise of their lock on distribution, the traditional copyright industries' central source of market power and profits has largely evaporated. To make matters worse, search engines and social media sites garner an increasing share of online advertising dollars as today's consumers look for content primarily through those portals rather than going directly to traditional media websites. In sum, even if there were no illicit file-sharing or streaming websites, the traditional copyright industries would face severe disruption in the face of new digital media. Digital distribution platforms radically alter the economics, efficiencies, and consumer expectations in markets for cultural expression.

Thus, market fundamentals likely spell the end of traditional copyright industry dominance regardless of whether massive copyright piracy can be squelched. But that does not mean that copyright law is less relevant in the digital era. Just the opposite: Copyright law plays a critical role in the competition between copyright industry incumbents and new digital media.

The reason is that new technologies push the boundaries of copyright law. Movie studios, record labels, print publishers, and authors' collective rights management organizations insist that their exclusive rights under copyright law extend to new ways for making content available to the public, using technologies that did not exist when the relevant provisions of the Copyright Act were enacted. Accordingly, they argue, new digital media must obtain copyright owner permission to exploit copyrighted content. In turn, new media respond that their uses of copyrighted content fall outside the parameters of copyright owners' exclusive rights. They insist that new digital media do not require permission from copyright owners, nor should permission be required.

In the face of legal uncertainties, numerous such questions arise: Must Facebook and Pinterest obtain copyright owner permission for users' postings of copyrighted material and user links to copyrighted content? Should news aggregation sites like Google News have to obtain licenses from newspaper publishers to display newspaper headlines and story leads even if the site links to the newspaper's website? Do Internet services that stream television broadcasts fall under Copyright Act provisions that give cable television companies a statutory license to retransmit broadcasts without having to obtain the broadcaster's permission? Under current copyright law, terrestrial radio stations need not obtain record label permission to broadcast recorded music. Should radio stations' online streaming of their broadcast feed enjoy the same benefit? What about webcasters like Pandora? Similarly, the two dominant music performance licensing organizations, ASCAP and BMI, are required, by decades-old antitrust decrees, to license all broadcasters, retail stores, and concert venues at reasonable rates, as determined by the presiding federal antitrust rate court. Do those antitrust decrees continue to make sense in an era of online music streaming dominated by technology giants Google, Apple, and Amazon?

The legal issues are complex, and we will unpack some of them below. But the same fundamental battle between copyright industries and new digital media underlies each such question—and many others. Copyright industries and traditional media regularly seek to use their copyrights in vast inventories of cultural expression to ward off new media competition—or to extract from new media as large a share of their revenue as possible. In the early twentieth century, composers and publishers of sheet music insisted that the then-nascent recording industry infringed their copyrights. In the mid-twentieth century, movie studios argued that community cable television operators infringed. In the late twentieth century, record labels set their sights on webcasters. And so on. In turn, new media often counter that their uses do not implicate copyright holder rights at all. Or new media argue that they fit within existing compulsory license regimes, entitling them to distribute copyright works without permission so long as they pay royalties at low rates set in antitrust rulings or administrative proceedings.

Are the battles over copyright only about digital technology?

No. Although digital technology has incited much of the current debate, the battles over copyright extend to other areas as well.

For example, the question of how long copyrights should last has been a lightning rod for controversy ever since the eighteenth-century "Battle of the Booksellers." British publishers of that era litigated for decades over whether authors held perpetual copyrights under common law. A group of London publishers claimed ownership of perpetual copyrights in classics of British literature. And they sued provincial publishers for infringement over reprint editions of those legacy works. Ultimately, the House of Lords ruled that, per the U.K. Statute of Anne of 1710, copyrights lasted at most twenty-eight years.

More recently, in response to copyright industry lobbying, Congress enacted the Copyright Term Extension Act of 1998 to add another twenty years to the copyright term—not only for works that had yet to be created but also for existing works that were already in copyright. Under the Copyright Term Extension Act, copyrights typically remain in force for the "life of the author plus 70 years," a period of time that can often last more than a century. A group of publishers and users of public domain works challenged the Act in court, arguing that it exceeded Congress' power under the Constitution, which authorizes exclusive rights for authors for "limited times." The challenge made its way to the Supreme Court. The Court's decision in *Eldred v. Ashcroft*,[7] issued in 2003, upheld Congress' power to lengthen the copyright term. But the Court intimated that the term extension might have been ill-advised. Indeed, as the next day's *New York Times* headline proclaimed, while *Eldred* was a "corporate victory" for the copyright industries who lobbied for the term extension, it "rais[ed] public consciousness" about copyright excess.[8] For many, the case tarnished the copyright industries as greedy and overreaching.

The copyright battles also extend, outside the realm of digital technology, to conflicts between authors. As noted above, writers, artists, and musicians have long plundered the works of their predecessors as raw material to create new expression. Yet today's copyright law sometimes stands in the way of such creative appropriation. In one monumental ruling, for example, a court held that rap musician Biz Markie had willfully infringed copyright when he digitally sampled a short snippet from a recording of the popular Gilbert O'Sullivan song, *Alone Again Naturally*. The court's ruling began with the biblical injunction, "Thou shall not steal" and concluded by referring the case to the U.S. Attorney for criminal prosecution.

Some musicians celebrate that ruling. For them, to "steal" even a single line from someone else's song is immoral conduct and bespeaks a lack of creativity. Other musicians retort that it can be highly creative to musically quote small snippets from previous work and that copyright law should permit such sampling. The same debate plays out in other art forms: Is it a copyright infringement for appropriation artists to incorporate images from existing paintings in their own work without the original artist's permission? For the publisher of *The Illustrated History of the Grateful Dead* to include thumbnail images of Grateful Dead concert posters in the book? For Harry Potter fans to create their own stories using Harry Potter characters, dialogue, and settings? For a documentary filmmaker to include copyrighted music, archival footage, and photographs from the late 1920s in a film about the stock market crash of 1929 without clearing the rights to those materials?

Digital technology greatly multiplies conflicts between authors. Every day, millions of amateur authors and social media users post their remixes and video memes of popular copyrighted content. They also repost, with a few added comments, copyrighted content they find online. But conflicts regarding creative appropriation abound offline as well. In either context, the question of whether a particular instance of creative appropriation amounts to copyright infringement typically depends on whether the appropriation qualifies as a fair use—a hotly contested defense to copyright infringement that we will explore below.

Finally, there are several longstanding debates about copyright law that embroil industries outside the Hollywood versus Silicon Valley axis. The question of whether copyright protection should extend to fashion design is one example.

And, more broadly, how, if at all, should copyright protection extend to functional designs of useful articles, such as chairs, bike racks, lamps, and mannequins? There is also a much litigated and hotly contested battle that is largely internal to Silicon Valley: How should copyright law apply to various elements of computer programs? And cutting across all of copyright, leading scholars argue that the test for copyright infringement—which is generally called "substantial similarity"—is in dire need of reform. As important as these—and other—debates are for copyright law and policy, this book focuses on the battles that have arisen between traditional copyright industries and new, digital media; the related debate about file sharing and private copying; and conflicts among authors spurred by digital technology.

III

WHY HAVE COPYRIGHT LAW?

Lying just under the surface of the debates that surround copyright law are sharp disagreements about what are the justifications, if any, for recognizing and protecting copyrights. Some observers and interested parties argue that copyrights need no policy justification because authors have an inherent right to control their own creations. Others maintain—in line with repeated Supreme Court pronouncements—that the copyright law serves primarily to benefit the public, and that any reward for authors is a secondary consideration. This chapter critically examines the leading rationales for copyright.

To benefit the public

As discussed in Chapter I, the Constitution's "Copyright Clause" provides Congress with the power (to exercise if it so chooses) "To promote the Progress of Science and useful Arts, by securing for limited Times to Authors and Inventors the exclusive Right to their respective Writings and Discoveries." The Copyright Clause thus authorizes Congress to enact a copyright law for a specific purpose: "to promote the Progress of Science" (with "useful Arts" being a reference to inventions that are the subject of patent law). In line with its original, eighteenth-century meaning, the word "science" is not limited to technical, hard sciences, but includes knowledge generally.

As the U.S. Constitution envisions, in other words, copyright law is meant to advance knowledge.

As such, the U.S. Constitution followed the model of the first copyright statute, the U.K.'s Statute of Anne of 1710, titled "An Act for the Encouragement of Learning." Indeed, the first copyright statute that Congress enacted under its new constitutional authority, the Copyright Act of 1790, was given that same title. The 1790 Act granted to U.S. citizens and residents who authored maps, navigational charts, or books the exclusive right to "print, reprint, publish, or vend" for a once-renewable fourteen-year term. By "books" the framers of the first copyright statute no doubt envisioned reference, instructional, and scientific texts. The political elite of the early republic generally disdained fiction and "light" entertainment. Hence, for them, copyright's central, if not sole, purpose was to further the diffusion of knowledge by providing authors with an incentive to produce enlightening and useful works—specifically maps, navigational charts, and books. Notably, the Copyright Act of 1790 also served the purpose of diffusing knowledge by sharply limiting the exclusive right granted to authors, most significantly by withholding any copyright protection for foreign works and thus leaving those works free for the taking.

Today, we no longer think of copyright protection as focused primarily on works of scholarship and instruction. Copyright, after all, also protects bubble gum pop songs, violent video games, amateur cat videos, Mickey Mouse cartoons, and even pornography. But, unlike the political elite at the founding of the United States, we celebrate having a plethora of creative expression that provides opinion, debate, inspiration, and entertainment, not just information and edification. In that light, the Supreme Court has stated repeatedly that copyright law's primary purpose is to benefit the public through promoting the creation and dissemination of creative expression. In the 1984 case of *Sony Corp. v. Universal City Studios*, the Supreme Court held that recording a television program for later viewing is fair use. In so holding, the Court gave the following rationale: "The monopoly privileges that Congress may authorize are neither unlimited nor primarily designed to provide a special private benefit. Rather, the limited grant is a means by which an important public purpose may be achieved. It is intended to motivate the creative activity of authors and inventors by the provision of a special reward, and to allow the public access to the products of their genius after the limited period of exclusive control has expired."

In other words, copyright serves the public benefit in the creation and dissemination of creative expression. In our day, that benefit lies in fostering expressive diversity and a lively sector of market-supported platforms and media for exchanging opinion, artistic expression, and entertainment. Copyright law serves that public purpose in two ways. First, it accords exclusive rights to authors to give them an incentive to create and disseminate their works. Second, copyright law limits those rights to further public access and to make it possible for today's creators to build upon the works of their predecessors.

Economic incentive

Closely tied to the public benefit rationale for copyright is the idea that copyrights provide an essential economic incentive for the creation and dissemination of original expression. To produce and disseminate creative expression costs time, labor, and money. Most obviously, perhaps, budgets for producing full-length motion pictures commonly run in the tens of millions of dollars. Costs include screenwriting, editing, cinematography, directing, paying actors, and the like. But once a movie is made, it costs very little to make a copy of it, or to share that copy with the entire world on a file-trading or online streaming site. If not for copyright, anyone could compete in the market for a popular movie by selling copies or streams. And since those competitors would not bear the substantial

costs of producing the movie in the first place, they could prof-
itably sell at a very low price (or even give away the movie for
free and look just to banner ads for revenue). In turn, if such
low price copies and streams of the movie are widely available to consumers, the studio that invested in creating and
producing the movie will not be able to charge enough to recover its costs. The studio can only hope to recover its production costs if it has exclusive rights to disseminate its movie and
if it can effectively enforce those rights.

Copyright's exclusive rights, in other words, serve to prevent what would otherwise be ruinous competition in the
market for copies of and access to creative works. Copyright's
exclusive rights thus enable authors, publishers, and studios
to recover their costs of creation—if the work is a commercial
success. And we care about that because creative works benefit the public. The economic incentive rationale for copyright
is based on a simple intuitive proposition: authors, publishers,
and studios who cannot hope to recover their costs of creation,
let alone earn a profit, will not produce and disseminate nearly
as much creative expression as we would like.

From the perspective of economics and social welfare,
however, granting exclusive rights in creative expression has
a dark side as well. Economists recognize that, once a work
has already been created, copyright causes fewer copies of
the work to be disseminated than would be the case in a fully
competitive market. If not for copyright, consumers could
buy copies at the very low competitive price. And follow-on
authors would not need to negotiate and pay expensive license fees to build on existing works in creating new expression. Because of copyright, however, copies of (or other access
to) a work cost more than the competitive price. Indeed, for
some works, the price is far higher than the competitive price.
And some consumers who would have purchased a copy at
the competitive price will not be able to afford that higher
price. Economists call that phenomenon "artificial scarcity"
or "deadweight loss," and recognize that it is an undesirable

result of copyright law. Copyright means that some members of the public will be deprived of access to existing works of original expression because they cannot or are not willing to pay the higher-than-competitive price for access.

In today's markets, the deadweight loss for consumers of popular movies, recorded music, books, and journalism seems minimal. Most American consumers can readily afford access to a broad menu of such works. There are multiple reasons for this. The Internet features a glut of available content, and new digital media happily supply copyright works as a loss leader for selling advertising and other goods. Competition from pirate sites might also weaken copyright industry's market power. Nonetheless, the deadweight loss for some works, notably scholarly books and journals, remains a serious problem. Libraries struggle to afford prices for those works. And for many in developing countries, the latest scholarship in medicine, hard sciences, and other disciplines is priced out of reach. Further, the cost of procuring copyright licenses and clearing rights remains a significant impediment to establishing universal libraries of books, movies, recorded music, and other works online. It also impedes today's authors from building on works of their predecessors that remain in copyright.

In any event, under the economic incentive model for copyright, deadweight loss is an unavoidable side effect of providing a necessary economic incentive for the creation of original expression. But the economic incentive approach still aims to minimize deadweight loss to the extent possible. Accordingly, the economic incentive approach teaches us that copyright should last only long enough and should accord exclusive rights that are only broad enough to provide the minimal economic incentive needed to spur the creation and dissemination of original expression. Otherwise, there is no justification for the deadweight loss that copyright imposes. Indeed, from an economic perspective, the widespread availability of cultural and informational works at a low price—or for free—is of great benefit to social welfare—provided, importantly, that the works would have been created and made available in the first place.

The economic incentive rationale for copyright has been criticized and defended on a number of fronts. Of particular relevance to the digital arena, commentators observe that millions of people create videos, photos, stories, poems, commentary, and music, and post those works online without any expectation of receiving financial remuneration through copyright law. Online social networks also make it possible for thousands of volunteers to cooperate in creating highly useful, complex works, ranging from Wikipedia to open source software such as Linux. And, of course, people have been creating stories, music, and art since time immemorial just for the joy of creating and sharing, without any need for copyright to provide an incentive for doing so.

Further, even for those who do wish to earn money from selling their creative works, digital technology has dramatically changed the equation for many types of works. Digital technology has vastly reduced the costs of producing many types of creative expression, obviating the need for expensive recording studios to produce quality sound recordings, for example. Social media also provide alternative means for creators to reach audiences, and the potential to benefit from free user recommendations rather than resorting to costly marketing campaigns in traditional media. Finally, digital technology opens up possibilities for creators to finance production without having to exert exclusive control over disseminating their works. Alternative financing sources that reduce dependence on copyright enforcement range from Kickstarter to advertising that is embedded in each copy or stream of a work, no matter who is disseminating it.

In short, if copyright were to disappear tomorrow, we would still have many more songs, videos, stories, and photographs created and posted online every day than any of us could possibly consume in a lifetime. Given that, does copyright's supposed economic incentive really justify its imposition of deadweight loss?

The economic incentive rationale provides a justification for copyright only to the extent that we benefit from having professional creators and certain types of expression that continue to rely on the economic incentive that copyright provides. Investigative journalism, full-length motion pictures, novels, nonfiction books, news and wildlife photography, and many other works typically demand a significant investment of time and money. We benefit greatly when skilled, creative authors are able to devote their full working time to producing such works. For some works, we also benefit from having intermediary organizations—publishers and studios—with the wherewithal and expertise to edit, augment, and generally bring authors' creations to fruition. Without copyright protection, we would expect to have far fewer of those especially costly works.

At bottom, then, copyright's economic incentive rationale makes sense only with respect to the creative works that would not otherwise be available without copyright protection. Especially costly works generally fall within that category— and those works provide us with significant public benefits. But from an economic incentive and public benefit perspective, to the extent that authors would create and disseminate original expression even without copyright protection (or with more narrow, shorter-term copyrights than copyright law currently provides), copyright law imposes socially wasteful deadweight loss without any countervailing benefit.

Copyright creates jobs and benefits the national economy

Arguments for why copyright must be rigorously enforced repeatedly invoke copyright's purported support for jobs and the national economy. A prime example: the International Intellectual Property Association (IIPA), a copyright industry trade association that lobbies for greater copyright protection and enforcement, periodically publishes reports titled *Copyright Industries in the U.S. Economy*. Industry briefs and congressional testimony frequently reference IIPA reports. The most recent report, published in 2016, concludes: "In 2015, the value added by the core copyright industries to U.S. GDP reached more than $1.2 trillion dollars ($1,235.6 billion), accounting for 11.69% of the U.S. economy. . . . The core copyright industries employed nearly 5.5 million workers in 2015, accounting for 3.87% of the entire U.S. workforce, and 4.57% of total private employment in the U.S."[1] The trade association report also trumpets copyright industries' contribution to the balance of trade. It states that "[s]ales of select U.S. copyright products in overseas markets amounted to $177 billion in 2015," a sum that, according the report, exceeds the respective exports of chemical, aerospace, agricultural, electrical equipment, and pharmaceutical products.[2] The U.S. Patent and Trademark Office and the Department of Commerce have cited similar figures, derived from industry reports, as evidence that strong copyright protection serves the national interest.[3]

Copyright industries and government agencies regularly highlight such figures to support expanding copyright protection and devoting additional resources to copyright enforcement. However, the figures must be met with healthy skepticism. First, according to IIPA reports, 75 percent of copyright exports consist of computer software industry revenues, with only 25 percent consisting of sales of cultural expression like movies, TV shows, books, and music.[4] The reports do not separate out the contributions of each sector to the domestic economy, but there is no reason to think that computer software industry revenue makes up less than the dominant share of that overall contribution as well. Computer software is protected by copyright, and software piracy has been a source of great concern among software producers. But to the extent movie studios, record labels, and publishers trot out IIPA figures regarding "core copyright industry" contributions to the national economy to support their lobbying efforts, those statements are misleading.

Second, the IIPA and government agency reports include within their definition of "core copyright industries" sectors that are partly or primarily users, not producers, of copyrighted content. For example, they include radio broadcasters even though broadcasters must acquire ASCAP and BMI licenses to broadcast musical compositions and vigorously oppose record labels' lobbying efforts to convince Congress to amend the Copyright Act to require broadcasters to pay record labels as well. Further, major software firms do not just produce copyrightable software. They also offer online intermediary Internet services—and, in that capacity, major software firms resist calls for imposing greater legal obligations on Internet service providers to police against copyright infringement.[5]

Third, the IIPA reports do not compare copyright industries' contribution to the national economy with that of the consumer technology, new media, and telecommunications sectors. The copyright industries insist that those businesses must bear the substantial burdens of policing for online copyright infringements. For example, the copyright industries lobby Congress to make the Internet service provider safe harbor conditional on Internet service provider filtering and policing. The copyright industries would also require new digital media to pay significantly greater copyright license fees for making cultural expression available to their customers.

Yet, the consumer technology, new media, and telecommunications sectors appear to provide a much larger contribution to the national economy than do cultural industries. According to the Telecommunications Industry Association, the market for goods and services for information and communications technologies amounted to $1.2 trillion in 2013.[6] That includes landlines, private networks, the Internet, wireless communications (including cellular and remote wireless sensors), and satellites—but not consumer technology (aside from wireless handsets) or new media. Another study concludes that the "Internet sector"—including provisioning of Internet backbone facilities, data storage, Internet access, cloud computing, search activities, social media, and other online markets—constituted 6 percent of the U.S. GDP in 2014.[7] Yet another report, issued by the Computer & Communications Industry Association, touts the contribution to the national economy of industries that depend on exceptions and limitations to copyright like the fair use doctrine. According to the report, in 2014 such "fair use industries" accounted for 16 percent of the economy, employed 1 in 8 workers, exported $368 billion in goods and services, and contributed $2.8 trillion to the GDP.[8]

Those figures—if they are to be believed any more than those of the IIPA—far exceed the size of the market for cultural expression. Indeed, they surpass the total economic contribution of all core copyright industries, even including computer software. Thus, to the extent that greater copyright protection imposes substantial costs on the telecommunications, new media, high tech, and other fair use–related industries, it might cause more harm than good for the national economy.

The industry-generated figures for the industries' relative contributions to the national economy are, no doubt, inflated on both sides. It is thus hard to assess the ramifications of those figures for copyright policy. In that vein, the U.S. Government Accountability Office has concluded that while intellectual property infringement clearly impacts particular industries, "it is difficult, if not impossible, to quantify the net effect of counterfeiting and piracy on the economy as a whole."[9] However, one thing is clear: any credible assessment of copyright's contribution to the national economy must take into account the costs as well as the benefits to the national economy of copyright protection and enforcement. Copyright enforcement that brings greater revenue to some U.S. industries but imposes equal or greater costs on others (if that is, in fact, the case) might not yield a net contribution to the U.S. economy.

Authors deserve to own what they create

The Supreme Court has repeatedly stated that copyright law serves to benefit the public and that any reward to the author is a secondary consideration. Nonetheless, the belief that authors inherently deserve to own and control what they create looms large among many creators and policymakers. Indeed, that belief predates modern copyright law, as expressed in the centuries-old dictum that one who profits from an author's work without the author's consent wrongfully reaps what he has not sown. In that view, authors have rights grounded in basic principles of justice or even the laws of nature, entirely independently from any copyright statute that a legislature might deem to enact.

Present-day authors and copyright industry spokespersons often draw upon that venerable idea. Consider, for example, the songwriter who insists that anyone who digitally samples a line from his song is "stealing" his creative product. Or authors and publishers who argue that Google is wrongfully profiting off authors' creative work when Google digitizes long out-of-print books to include in a searchable database. Those are essentially natural rights arguments. They posit that authors have an inherent exclusive right to prevent others from copying their work. In that view, the Copyright Act serves—or should serve—fundamentally to secure and protect authors' preexisting, inherent right; it does not merely grant to authors a limited monopoly in order to benefit the public.

In the Anglo-American copyright tradition, the idea that authors have inherent, natural rights drew inspiration from John Locke's labor-desert theory of property. Locke posited that individuals earn the right to appropriate a previously unowned material object from nature by "mingling" it with their physical labor and improving it to create a value-added version of the object. Under Locke's theory of property, for example, a carpenter who gathers driftwood from a public beach and then carves and polishes it to make a coffee table would deserve a property right in the table by virtue of adding value to the driftwood through his labor. And in Locke's imagination, such rights arose in the state of nature, even before governments enacted property laws.

Drawing from Locke's paradigm, proponents of a natural law copyright posit that authors are, if anything, even more entitled to property in their creations than are physical laborers. An author's expression, they argue, is an ideal object, a "product of his mind," which the author enjoys the right to hold as his property by virtue of having created it with his mental labor. Further, authors' creations arise entirely in the author's mind. They would not exist at all but for the author's intellectual labor.

Locke's theory has always been an undercurrent in American copyright law. Indeed, Eaton S. Drone, the author of the leading copyright treatise of the late nineteenth century, argued that authors have a perpetual property right in their creations, a natural right that the copyright statute wrongfully takes away when it imposes a limited copyright term. Nonetheless, U.S. copyright law has traditionally reflected the dominant public benefit rationale rather than the natural rights, labor-desert undercurrent. To Eaton Drone's and his followers' dismay, U.S. copyright acts have always limited the copyright term. Further, until the late twentieth century, U.S. copyright law required that authors affirmatively claim their copyrights by affixing a copyright notice. Indeed, authors were required to make their work available to the public as a condition of copyright protection, both by publishing the work and by depositing copies with the Library of Congress (and its predecessors). In addition, U.S. copyright law did not protect foreign works at all until 1891. All these restrictions and conditions cut against the notion that U.S. copyright law has traditionally recognized an author's natural right.

Having said that, however, since enactment of the Copyright Act of 1976, U.S. copyright law does bear at least some influence of the authors' rights tradition. That tradition views authors' rights as inherent property and personality rights. With roots in Continental Europe, it has dominated the copyright jurisprudence of many countries outside the United States. Importantly, it is also reflected in key provisions of the world's premier multilateral copyright treaty, the Berne Convention for the Protection of Literary and Artistic Works. The United States joined the Berne Convention in 1989, and the Copyright Act of 1976 was drafted with the goal of moving the United States toward compliance with Berne. The Berne Convention forbids the imposition of any formalities, such as a copyright notice, as a requirement for copyright protection. It also forbids discrimination against foreign authors. Further, it sets a minimum copyright term as the life of the author plus fifty years, which, while not perpetual, is still considerably longer than the copyright term in effect in the United States prior to the Copyright Act of 1976. It is possible, although probably not capable of being empirically tested, that changes in U.S. copyright law to comport with the Berne Convention have bolstered the belief in authors' natural rights among some authors, commentators, and policymakers in this country.

Copyright scholars have presented cogent arguments, drawing on the natural rights philosophies of John Locke and others, for why a careful reading of authors' natural rights theory actually imposes sharp limits on authors' exclusive copyrights.[10] But, like Eaton Drone, many who believe that authors have inherent property rights in their creative product insist that copyrights should last longer and should be more robust and absolute—and that anyone who copies or profits from an author's work without the author's permission is acting immorally.

It would take us too far afield to delve into whether natural rights theory supports a limited or absolute property right in authors' creations. What is important to remember is that even if authors do have some kind of inherent right, no individual rights are absolute in U.S. law or, indeed, in the law of any country. All rights must sometimes give way before other individuals' rights and/or the public interest. As propounded in the often-cited axiom of Oliver Wendell Holmes, Jr., my right of free speech—fundamental as it might be—does not give me the right of "falsely shouting fire in a crowded theater." Likewise, even countries that avowedly embrace authors' rights impose limits on those rights to ensure that others can copy and build on existing works in certain circumstances and at some point in time. Indeed, many of the same battles over copyright that we explore in this book also reverberate in Germany, France, and other so-called authors' rights countries.

Authors have the personal right to control what they create

Another version of authors' natural rights is the view that authors have an inherent right to control the form and manner in which their work is communicated to the public. This perceived right, which has roots in the writing of the German idealist philosopher Immanuel Kant, is less a property right than a personal right. Proponents emphasize that creators have a deep personal connection to their creative work. Accordingly, to distort a creator's work or to communicate it without correct authorship attribution amounts to a personal harm, somewhat like that caused by defamation or invasion of privacy.

The view that authors have a personal right of creative control undergirds moral rights protection outside the United States. As discussed in Chapter I, moral rights give authors the legal right to control the timing and manner in which their creative work is disseminated to the public, independently from the right to exploit the work economically. Moral rights, and the personalist conception of authorship that underlies them, have traditionally been regarded as antithetical to U.S. copyright law. Indeed, although the Berne Convention requires protection for authors' moral rights of integrity and attribution, the United States has protected those rights grudgingly and parsimoniously. Nonetheless, like the view that authors have an inherent right of literary property, the idea that authors have a personal right of creative control surfaces from time to time in debates over copyright law and policy.

IV

FAIR USE

Fair use is a longstanding, major exception to copyright owners' exclusive rights. You do not infringe copyright if your copying of someone else's work qualifies as fair use. I explained some fair use basics in Chapter I. Recall that to determine whether a given use of copyrighted material is fair use, courts analyze the facts and equities of each case in light of four statutory factors. The court may also consider other factors that it deems relevant.

We now dig deeper into fair use doctrine and look at some of the much-debated issues regarding fair use.

Which uses qualify as fair use?

No use categorically qualifies as fair use. Courts have discretion to determine fair use on a case-by-case basis, relying on the four statutory factors as guidelines for decision. Thus, fair use doctrine is flexible. It enables courts to apply fair use to new technologies and uses.

Yet, fair use's open-ended, flexible character does not mean that fair use case law lacks predictable precedential rules. Most significantly, recall that if a court finds that a use is transformative, that typically counts very heavily in favor of fair use. A transformative use is one that has a fundamentally different purpose or character than the copyrighted work that the defendant copied. Hence, one must compare the alleged infringer's use with the copied work to determine whether the use is transformative. To copy a 1950s print advertisement in a non-fiction historical commentary on post-war advertising would be a transformative use. To copy the same advertisement to use it in a new advertisement would not.

Courts have found many different types of uses to be transformative in the particular context of the case before them. These have included copying for the purpose of artistic expression, parody, criticism, social satire, biography, history, litigation, education, research, and providing information location or search tools.

The commercial or noncommercial character of the use also bears upon whether the use qualifies as fair use. If the defendant's use is noncommercial, that weighs in favor of fair use. But the commercial character of the use is not definitive. Courts have found numerous commercial uses to be fair use, generally when the use is not only commercial but also transformative. On the other hand, courts have sometimes held that nontransformative uses that we would not ordinarily think of as commercial, such as downloading copyrighted songs from the Internet for personal use, are in fact "commercial" and do not qualify as fair use.

If the defendant copied only a small portion of the copyrighted work, that can also count in favor of fair use. However, that factor is not determinative either. Courts have held repeatedly that a defendant may copy as much as reasonably necessary for a transformative purpose—and numerous cases have recognized that it may sometimes be reasonably necessary to copy the entire work. At the same time, even copying a small portion might count against fair use if that portion is qualitatively significant for the copyrighted work. In *Harper & Row Publishers v. Nation Enterprises*, the Supreme Court famously held that *The Nation* magazine's copying of some 300 words from former president Gerald Ford's 200,000-word manuscript was not fair use, in part because those 300 words were the dramatic heart of Ford's book. In short, contrary to some popular misconceptions, there is no magic number of words or notes that may be copied and that necessarily will qualify as fair use.

Finally, while transformative purpose is almost universally a *sufficient* condition for fair use (so long as the defendant has copied only what is reasonably necessary for that purpose), transformative use is not a *necessary* condition for a finding of fair use. For example, courts have found that recording television programs for later viewing may be fair use even though that is not a transformative use. Likewise, posting portions of books on a university's electronic course reserves and rendering books accessible to visually disabled readers have been held to be fair use even though the court declined to categorize them as transformative. The question of when nontransformative uses may qualify as fair use remains a contested area of copyright law.

Have courts always given so much weight to whether the defendant's use is "transformative"?

No. The question of the transformativeness of the use has not always dominated fair use doctrine. Notably, the Supreme Court stated in 1985 in *Harper & Row Publishers v. Nation Enterprises* that the single most important factor in fair use analysis is the effect of the use upon the potential market for the copyrighted work. But the Supreme Court subsequently reversed course. It held in 1994, in *Campbell v. Acuff-Rose Music, Inc.*, that market harm is just one of the four fair use factors, to be weighed together with the others. Indeed, the Court held in *Campbell* that special consideration should be given to whether the allegedly infringing use is "transformative." In so holding, the Court stated that "the goal of copyright, to promote science and the arts, is generally furthered by the creation of transformative works."

Even following *Campbell*, it took several years for the transformative use doctrine to take root in the lower courts. But today, courts rarely question the centrality of whether the use is transformative—and that issue generally dominates over whether the use causes market harm. If the court finds that the allegedly infringing use is transformative, it will almost always find that the use is a fair use, unless the defendant copied more than reasonably necessary for the use. At the same time, even nontransformative uses can sometimes qualify as fair use.

What is the debate regarding the transformative use doctrine?

Some critics of current fair use doctrine argue that market harm, not the transformative character of the defendant's use, should still govern fair use. They contend that copyright holders should have the prerogative to decide to whom to license uses of their works and at what price. And, they argue, it should not matter whether the use is transformative. Absent special circumstances preventing the parties from negotiating a copyright license, copying should never qualify as fair use.

More specifically, some commentators have argued that fair use doctrine's great solicitude toward transformative uses undermines authors' exclusive right to make derivative works based on their creative expression. If merely transforming an author's work is enough to qualify for fair use, what is left of the authors' exclusive right to modify, adapt, and make sequels to their works?

Until recently, that argument was a red herring. Courts almost universally defined "transformative" as using the copyrighted work for a fundamentally different expressive purpose, not modifying it for the same expressive purpose. Hence, scanning books in their entirety, without modification, to build a database for online search is transformative. So is making a parody of a copyrighted work. But simply making a Hollywood movie sequel of another Hollywood movie for the same entertainment purpose is not transformative, even if the defendant's sequel contains significant new creative expression and copies none of the dialogue of the underlying work.

Recently, however, a couple of courts have muddied the waters. In particular, the court in *Cariou v. Prince* held that appropriation artist Richard Prince's alteration of Patrick Cariou's copyrighted photographs in some of Prince's paintings and collages was transformative fair use. The court reasoned that "Prince's images . . . have a different character, give Cariou's photographs a new expression, and employ new aesthetics with creative and communicative results distinct from Cariou's."[1] That court's ruling is particularly controversial because Prince's expressive purpose was avowedly the same as Cariou's—to create an artistic work. Prince expressly disavowed any intention to criticize or comment on Cariou's work. Further, the court gave little guidance as to how distinct a defendant's "new aesthetics" must be to qualify as transformative fair use.

If distinct aesthetics are truly enough to qualify as fair use, does the fair use defense indeed swallow up the copyright holder's exclusive right to make modified versions of a copyrighted work? Or should using a copyright work as raw material for a very different creative work of the same genre—such as digitally sampling a single line from a recorded song—qualify as transformative fair use even if the overall expressive purpose is the same?

It remains to be seen how courts will answer that question. Also uncertain is whether courts will generally follow the *Cariou* ruling or return to the different-expressive-purpose understanding of transformative use. It is even possible that courts will react to *Cariou* by reducing the weight given to the transformative nature of the defendant's use. One appellate court has already expressed support for reinvigorating the importance of the market harm factor.

Is personal copying fair use?

There is no settled answer that applies to all personal copying.

In 1984, in *Sony Corp. v. Universal City Studios*, the Supreme Court held that consumer recordings of television programs for later viewing—what the Court termed "time-shifting"—are fair use. Observers have since debated how broadly that holding should be interpreted. Copyright industry spokespersons have insisted that *Sony* should be overturned as wrongly decided. Alternatively, they argue, *Sony* should be limited to its bare facts—recording free over-the-air broadcasting using analog recording equipment that consumers cannot easily use to skip commercials. By contrast, consumer advocates have argued, with some lower court support, that *Sony* stands for the proposition that when consumers are entitled to access content on one device, it is fair use for them to copy it for their own viewing or listening on other devices—what courts have termed "space-shifting." Indeed, some commentators argue that all noncommercial personal copying is fair use.

Recent lower court rulings have rejected the most extreme positions on both sides. On one hand, courts have applied *Sony* more expansively than the copyright industry would like. They have held that it is fair use to record television programs using digital video recorders that consumers can program to automatically skip commercials. In addition, a lower court recently ruled that Dish Network's Hopper service, which enables Dish subscribers to view their recorded programming at different times on multiple devices, constitutes noncommercial time-shifting and space-shifting, which, the court stated, "is paradigmatic fair use under existing law." On the other hand, contrary to some commentators' calls to immunize all personal copying, courts have held that individuals' downloading of songs for their personal enjoyment from peer-to-peer file-sharing platforms infringes copyright and is not fair use.

To copy songs, movies, or TV programs that I have already purchased is arguably quite different from downloading infringing copies from peer-to-peer file-sharing platforms. Yet despite consumer-friendly lower court rulings, it remains a matter of debate whether engaging in such space-shifting is fair use. Indeed, the Supreme Court has left open the question of whether a consumer's copying of his videos and music onto a cloud server for later streaming to himself renders the consumer and/or cloud server provider liable for copyright infringement. Copyright industry spokespersons sometimes say that such uses are not fair use, but merely "tolerated uses." In other words, the industries have no current plans to sue individuals for personal space-shifting of content that the individual has legally acquired. But they reserve the right to litigate the issue in the future.

Why have fair use?

Fair use enhances creative expression, protects freedom of speech, and, arguably, fosters technological innovation for personal copying.

Under the market-centered approach to fair use that the Supreme Court championed in *Harper & Row Publishers v. Nation Enterprises*, fair use was understood to be an anomalous exception to the copyright holder's exclusive rights. In *Harper & Row* the Court characterized fair use as an equitable doctrine "predicated on the author's implied consent to 'reasonable and customary' use." In other words, fair use should be available only when the copyright holder would be expected to consent to the use but is prevented from doing so because the cost of negotiating for a license would far exceed any reasonable license fee that the user would pay for the use in question.

With the rise of the transformative use approach to fair use, however, that constricted reading has been soundly rejected. Building on *Campbell v. Acuff-Rose Music, Inc.*, courts now view fair use as a doctrine that serves the same purposes as copyright law generally. Under current jurisprudence, fair use carves out a breathing space for unrestricted transformative uses of existing copyrighted works. These range from scanning millions of books to include in the Google Books database to authors' creative reformulation and remixing of existing expression in creating new works (so long as the author's expressive purpose, conception, or message is deemed to be sufficiently different from that of the underlying copyrighted work). In other words, like copyright protection generally, fair use promotes the production and dissemination of creative expression, information, and commentary.

Indeed, the Supreme Court has recognized that fair use serves as a safeguard for freedom of speech within copyright law. If not for fair use, copyright law would abridge freedom of speech because it would unduly burden the ability of speakers to convey their messages using cultural works that audiences recognize and understand. It would also hinder copying from existing works in order to parody or criticize those works or their authors. Moreover, but for fair use, copyright law would frequently stand in the way of copying existing works for purposes of scholarship, education, information location, and news reporting. Fair use thus furthers the goals of the First Amendment as well as of copyright law.

Finally, to the extent fair use applies to personal copying—an issue discussed in the previous question—it both carves out a space for individuals to enjoy creative expression on multiple devices and makes it possible for technology industries to produce new consumer copying platforms and devices without fear of facing copyright infringement liability. As I will discuss in Chapter V, a manufacturer that provides a platform or device that consumers use to copy copyrightable expression might face liability for consumers' infringements unless consumers' copying qualifies as fair use.

V

CURRENT CONTROVERSIES

Does file sharing really harm authors and copyright industries?

The copyright industries insist that file sharing (via both downloading and streaming) poses a major threat to their future viability. Underlying that concern, the industries—and many observers—posit that individuals who can freely enjoy music and video online without payment are much less likely to buy such content. In support, the industries point to the fact that the emergence of peer-to-peer file sharing of music at the turn of the millennium coincided with a dramatic decline in recording industry revenues.

Nonetheless, the impact of file sharing is the subject of debate. A number of studies conclude that file sharing has actually resulted in little or no harm to copyright industry revenues. There are several possible explanations for this counterintuitive finding. First, contrary to some highly exaggerated industry claims, most consumer copying and file sharing is not a substitute for purchasing. The notion that the average teenager who illegally downloads a thousand songs would actually purchase any more than a fraction of those songs if only he were prevented from downloading illegally is nothing short of fantasy.

Second, some recent studies conclude that individuals who trade infringing music on peer-to-peer file-sharing platforms are also heavy consumers of legal media—indeed, that such file sharers "buy as many or more legal DVDs, CDs, and sub-scription media services as their non-file-sharing, Internet-using counterparts."[1] Widespread exposure to music and movies via illegal channels might also spur demand for related goods and services, such as concert tickets, band merchandise, and theatrical exhibitions of movies.

Third, there are alternative explanations for the downturn in the recording industry. Record labels garnered substantial profits from consumers' conversion of their record collections from vinyl to CDs in the years immediately preceding the emergence of file sharing. Hence, the labels' subsequent de-cline was at least in part a return to normal. Their decline also reflects the unbundling of the record album, as consumers buy access only to the individual songs they wish to hear. Indeed, today, even legal music platforms, such as digital download and streaming services like iTunes and Spotify, generate less revenue for record labels than did the labels' CD cash cow.

By contrast, other studies, conducted before the emer-gence of licensed music streaming services, concluded that file sharing caused a displacement of roughly 30 percent of recorded music sales. Some studies also suggest that file sharing's impact on copyright industry revenues might differ from industry to industry and even within industries. The im-pact on a given industry depends on the rate of declining pro-duction costs due to digital technology and the availability of legal copies, online streaming, and other forms of access in that industry. One study concluded, for example, that consumer movie downloads from pirate BitTorrent portals harm the for-eign market for theatrical releases of new movies, but not the U.S. box office. The reason is that new Hollywood movies can take several weeks to appear on movie theater screens in for-eign countries, and foreign consumers are unwilling to wait that long to see new movies.[2]

A 2015 study prepared for the European Commission found, similarly, that illegal downloads and streaming displace sales for newly released hit movies but that there is no robust statistical evidence that online infringements displace sales of music, books, video games, television series, or older movies.[3] The 2015 study also suggests that, at least for the music industry, illegal downloads and streaming might shift industry profit centers rather than resulting in net revenue displacement. It found that illegal music downloads and streams spur greater live concert attendance and that increased concert revenues appear to compensate for displaced CD sales.[4]

At bottom, file sharing's impact on copyright industry revenues is rapidly changing and is thus difficult to measure. Studies assessing the extent to which illicit file-trading substitutes for CD and DVD sales have diminished relevance in today's home entertainment markets. Today, legal digital downloads and streaming have surpassed CD and DVD sales as the primary source of home entertainment revenue for record labels and studios. Therefore, the more relevant question today is whether illicit file trading and streaming depress prices for legal downloads and streaming service subscriptions, not whether they substitute for CD and DVD sales.

Authorized download and streaming platforms earn revenue from a combination of advertising and consumer purchases and subscriptions. Either way, they must compete with illicit platforms that do not pay license fees to copyright owners and that supply content to consumers for free. The availability of illicit platforms likely drives down the price that consumers are willing to pay for licensed downloads and streaming subscriptions, and that advertisers are willing to pay for advertising on licensed platforms. In turn, licensed download and streaming platforms might be willing to pay less for copyright licenses than they would absent illicit competition.

However, it's not clear to what extent, if any, illicit platforms impact authorized download and streaming services. Certainly, there are indications that the growing popularity of licensed online streaming services—like Spotify,

Apple Music, YouTube, Tidal, Amazon Music and Video, and Netflix—has coincided with dramatically diminished consumer demand for pirated content. Indeed, licensed music streaming—which now accounts for 62 percent of the U.S. music business—has recently contributed to a significant rebound in music industry revenues.[5] Apparently, a good part of the demand for infringing file sharing stems from consumers' desire to have immediate access to whatever music, movies, and television programs they want, not necessarily to have access for free. Studies show that consumers' desire to obtain content that is not available legally contributes significantly to illegal downloading and streaming.[6] And conversely, consumers are willing to pay modest subscription fees and/or suffer the inconvenience of advertising for licensed streaming services that offer access to vast catalogues of popular works.

Today, music streaming services seem to provide the functional equivalent of universal catalogues. Further, music streaming services both charge subscription prices that many consumers are willing to pay and offer advertiser-supported versions that require no direct monetary payment from users. As a result, they increasingly serve as an attractive alternative to illegal downloading and streaming.

By contrast, video streaming services have far more limited offerings. And a recent study found that current prices for legal online access for films and TV series are higher than those that the vast majority of illegal downloaders and streamers would be willing to pay.[7] As a result, illicit file sharing of movies and television shows through BitTorrent and storage locker sites continues to involve millions of users and to claim a large percentage of web traffic overall. If studios were to join record labels in making all the content they control widely available to streaming services—and to do so at lower prices—it seems that consumers would flock to those services in greater numbers, enabling the studios to compete quite well against infringing file sharing.

Of course, that still begs the question of whether and to what extent illicit file sharing and streaming platforms depress revenues that copyright industries could otherwise earn from licensed streaming services. Online video streaming services offering universal catalogues may well diminish demand for illicit video sites, as has happened with music. But if licensed services charge more than consumers otherwise disposed to illegal streaming would be willing to pay, those consumers would likely migrate back to illicit platforms. Put another way, so long as illicit platforms remain a consumer option, that threat likely imposes limits on how high a price licensed streaming services can charge. Hence, to the extent that higher prices for copyright licensed streaming services would dampen consumer demand for those services, competition from illicit platforms likely depresses revenues that copyright industries could earn but for that illicit competition.

In any event, even if file sharing has negatively impacted copyright industry revenues, the industries appear to remain vibrant and vital, both in terms of overall productivity and revenues. Whatever file sharing's impact on per unit profitability of new record albums, many more albums have been released each year since the advent of file sharing than previously. Likewise, the number of annual feature film releases increased from 2003 and 2007 before slumping thereafter. Granted, that post-2007 decline could be attributable to increased movie piracy made possible by greater bandwidth. But it also coincides with a substantial increase in television show production.[8] Further, copyright industry data indicate that in every year from 2003 through 2015 (the latest year for which the industry presents figures), U.S. copyright industry growth consistently outpaced the rest of the economy (although those figures lump together software with cultural industries).[9]

A similar picture seems to emerge in other countries. As the U.K. government-commissioned Hargreaves Report iterated:

"We conclude that many creative businesses are experiencing turbulence from digital copyright infringement, but that at the level of the whole economy, measurable impacts are not as stark as is sometimes suggested."[10]

In sum, there is incomplete, contradictory data about the impact of unlicensed file sharing—both downloading and streaming—on copyright industries. If we measure file sharing's impact by the extent to which file sharing actually substitutes for sales of licensed copies or streaming services, the impact seems to be quite modest—except for when it comes to newly released, top-selling movies. Nonetheless, our assessment of file sharing's impact must ultimately be based largely on counterfactual hypotheses. What, we must ask, would licensed streaming and download services be able to charge if they did not have to compete with free illicit file sharing and streaming? Further, to what extent is consumers' embrace of legal streaming a result of studios' and labels' ongoing campaigns to shut down illicit sites? In other words, what would be the harm to copyright industry revenues if unlicensed file sharing and streaming were simply allowed to flourish without hindrance? In that latter scenario, it is plausible to assume that massive illicit file sharing would displace copyright industry revenues to a significantly greater extent than seems to be the case today.

If file sharing harms copyright industries, can't they just adjust their business models?

Copyright industry critics argue that the industries can and should change their business models rather than expending enormous resources in trying to stamp out file sharing and forcibly enlisting Internet intermediaries to police against online infringement. In support, the critics note that copyright industry lobbyists have repeatedly exaggerated the threat that new media and consumer copying technologies pose to the copyright system.

There is much to that criticism. Incumbent copyright industries have insisted time and time again that new copying and distribution media, ranging from player piano rolls to home video recorders, will spell the death of creativity as we know it unless Congress and the courts give copyright holders a veto over any use of their content by new media. Perhaps most dramatically, in 1982 Jack Valenti, then-president of the Motion Picture Association of America (MPAA), declared in congressional testimony: "I say to you that the VCR is to the American film producer and the American public as the Boston strangler is to the woman home alone." Yet despite Valenti's dire predictions that consumers' recording of television shows posed a mortal threat to television and movie studios, the studios profited immensely from the VCR and its digital descendant, the DVR. Indeed, before peaking in 2004, DVD sales became the primary source of motion picture industry profits, exceeding revenues from theatrical exhibitions.

Critics insist that apocalyptic warnings of copyright industries' demise at the hands of massive, unrestricted piracy are one more instance of the boy crying wolf. Just as the motion picture industry managed to turn home recording equipment into a major profit center, so can today's industries devise ways to prosper in an era of free file sharing. In the critics' view, digital technology and computer networks create opportunities as well as minefields for the copyright industries. They drastically reduce industry costs in production and distribution, and offer new avenues for reaching audiences. If the industries cannot take advantage of those opportunities, they deserve to face extinction.

However, the story of VCRs and the motion picture industries' subsequent success in marketing movies on video and DVD is not really an apt analogy to massive illicit copying, streaming, and distribution over the Internet. Unlike illicit file sharing, VCRs did not provide a platform through which millions of individuals could create and disseminate perfect copies of motion pictures and television shows at virtually no marginal cost. Further, at the motion picture industry's insistence, digital video recorders and DVDs came packaged with digital rights management technology that hindered large-scale consumer copying. By contrast, illicit file sharing enables individuals (and commercial pirates) to be distributors of perfect copies (or streams) of movies, TV programs, recorded music, and books in direct competition with copyright holders' core markets. Hence, whatever harm illicit file sharing actually causes copyright industry revenues—and recall that evidence of that harm is mixed—we can assume that it is far greater than that caused by analog home copying equipment.

Of necessity, studios, record labels, and publishers compete with free file sharing. To that end, they must presumably lower their prices and licensing rates for online platforms as needed to compete with illegal copies and streaming. Alternatively, the industries could attempt to use their content as a "loss leader." In other words, they could underprice their content or give it away for free in order to spur sales of complementary goods or services. That is roughly the model of Apple's iTunes, which sells digital music downloads quite cheaply as a loss leader for marketing its mobile devices. Along those lines, copyright industries could morph into niche providers of supplemental services—like live performances, readings, merchandising, and theatrical exhibitions—that cannot be readily copied or streamed without permission. The copyright industries might also turn to an advertiser-supported business model for monetizing file sharing. I address that possibility in the next question.

If movie and television studios, record labels, and print publishers must adjust to copyright piracy by changing their business model, the copyright industries as we know them might shrink to a pale shadow of what they are today. Certainly, it is understandable why the industries resist the severe disruption to their business that file sharing might portend and why they lobby for greater copyright enforcement to prevent it.

Yet, digital technology spells the end of copyright industries' traditional business models even aside from the impact of illicit copying and streaming. As discussed in Chapter II, incumbent copyright industries have lost their monopoly over the distribution of cultural expression. They now face competition from new digital media that are more effective, efficient, and user-friendly in aggregating and disseminating content online.

In a market economy, companies earn profits that are more or less commensurate with the value that they bring to the table. Movie and television studios, record labels, and print publishers undoubtedly continue to play a vital role in producing, packaging, editing, and distributing much highly valued creative expression. But they are not dominant players in the mushrooming market of online distribution. It thus seems inevitable that new digital media will garner a significant share of the revenue pie from disseminating cultural expression—and might gobble up traditional copyright industries in the process.

In short, copyright industries are facing fundamental challenges to their core business resulting from digital technology, and they will continue to face those challenges even if piracy can be substantially dampened. Effective copyright enforcement against illicit file sharing and commercial pirate platforms is warranted. But copyright law should not serve as a tool for incumbent copyright industries to protect their traditional business models from competition from technology companies and new media that provide valuable digital distribution services.

Would it be best for copyright industries to monetize file sharing through advertising rather than trying to stamp it out?

Possibly. Major studios, record labels, and authors' collective rights management organizations have already moved in that direction on some social media. YouTube's Content ID content identification system is a notable example. Recall that YouTube gives copyright holders a choice to monetize or remove videos that Content ID, using copyright holder-supplied metadata, flags as potentially infringing. Google reports that its Content ID system has almost entirely replaced DMCA notice and take-down on YouTube.[11] According to Google, over 98 percent of copyright management on YouTube now takes place through Content ID, while only 2 percent of allegedly infringing videos are subject to takedown notices. In addition, when Content ID flags user-posted videos as potentially infringing, copyright owners elect to monetize that content through advertising more than 95 percent of the time. Copyright owners choose to remove infringing videos in only a small fraction of cases. In other words, copyright holders almost always tolerate YouTube users' postings of content that are flagged as potentially infringing. Rather than removing potentially infringing postings, they generally choose to earn revenue (shared with YouTube) from targeted advertising that appears alongside the user-posted videos. Facebook's use of Audible Magic and Rights Manager seems to work in similar fashion, although Facebook has not released data regarding how often rights holders monetize rather than block content posted on that social media platform. So does the use of Audible Magic's automated content identification system by video-sharing sites Vimeo and Dailymotion.

At bottom, then, assuming the YouTube experience is indicative of that of other large social media platforms, copyright industries have come to countenance and monetize vast amounts of user sharing of copyright industry content online. In turn, social media users are free, by and large, to post popular music recordings and scenes from movies and TV shows without fear that their posts will be taken down or that they will be sued for copyright infringement. The same is true regarding remixes that incorporate copyrighted content within user-created expression. Even when an automated content identification system flags such user-created derivative works as infringing, the user remix almost always remains on the social media platform, free for all users to view. At the same time, advertising revenues generated by the remix are typically shared by the social media platform and the owner of the copyright in movie, TV show, or recorded music that the user incorporates in his or her remix.

Perhaps a similar accommodation could be instituted for BitTorrent streaming and file trading. An advertiser-supported tolerance for user infringement might be feasible if copyright holders are able to embed advertising within their works—through product placement, for example—or if embedded software code could trigger advertising on viewers' and listeners' screens. After all, companies that pay for advertising might not care who distributes their ads, or how their ads are distributed, so long as more potential consumers view them.

Consequently, might embedded and targeted advertising be a win-win solution to the battle between copyright industries and those who foster and participate in file sharing? On balance, the move toward advertising seems to offer significant advantages over a universe in which copyright industries engage in a protracted, costly, and likely futile campaign to stamp out file sharing. However, advertising is far from a perfect solution.

From the copyright industry perspective, it depends largely on the bottom line. Do the social media and content sharing sites produce enough advertising revenue for copyright owners to make such arrangements worthwhile? Social media platform payments have become a major source of revenue for rights holders. But rights holders argue that social media take advantage of the Internet service provider safe harbor—which gives user-generated content platforms immunity from infringement liability as long as they comply with notice and takedown—to pay far less than what rights holders' permission to stream millions of copyrighted songs and videos content is worth.

Granted, social media platforms like YouTube and Facebook currently negotiate with the copyright industries from a position of relative strength, in which social media's identification and filtering of potentially infringing user postings are voluntary. Record labels insist, accordingly, that YouTube is able "to offer a below-market rate and say 'take it or leave it,'" knowing that record labels and songwriters must accept YouTube's offer or spend countless hours sending takedown notices only to find unauthorized copies popping back up on YouTube soon after they are removed.[12] YouTube retorts that it now pays the music industry more than $1 billion per year in license fees, and that it pays at a higher rate than Spotify and Pandora (which do not fall within the Internet service provider safe harbor because they select and upload recorded music for streaming to subscribers rather than hosting user-posted content).[13]

The record label's claim that YouTube pays a "below-market rate" is circular and nonsensical. True, the market rate is partly a function of which party has the burden of policing for infringements under copyright law—and, currently, the law imposes that burden on the copyright owners. Thus, if Congress were to amend copyright law to require social media to police and filter out infringing content or else face liability for their users' infringements, copyright holders would, indeed, gain a somewhat stronger hand in bargaining with YouTube and other social media platforms for a higher share of advertising revenue. Whether that change in the law would then yield licensing fees at the true "market rate" or, rather, an "above-market rate" depends on what one thinks the legal rule should be to begin with.

Moreover, even a change in the law would not alter the fundamental economics of the market. YouTube and Facebook are immensely valuable distribution channels for any songwriter or record label—and, for that matter, any movie or TV studio—wanting to reach a mass, global audience. YouTube and Facebook also bring their time-honed expertise and massive user data required for lucrative targeted advertising. Of course, the social media giants also bring the advertisers themselves. Hence, in a competitive market—short of collusion among all rights holders—it is doubtful that a change in the law that requires YouTube and Facebook to institute automatic content identification systems like those that the social media giants have already voluntarily implemented would dramatically improve rights holders' bargaining position.[14] The days in which the labels and studios dominated content distribution—and could thus earn a large premium for distributing as well as producing content—are gone. In any event, YouTube has recently signed long-term agreements with three record labels and their associated music publishers—Universal Music Group, Song Music Entertainment, and Warner Music Group—establishing better royalty rates for the labels and permitting YouTube to introduce a new paid music service akin to Apple Music and Spotify Premium.[15]

From the vantage point of social media users, advertiser-supported permission to post copyrighted content might appear to be an ideal, costless option. Yet, advertising is not really free. Granted, we need not make monetary payments to watch or listen to advertiser-supported content on social media—anymore than we need to pay out of our wallets to listen to advertiser-supported broadcast radio. But we pay in other ways. We pay with the time and attention that advertising demands of us. We also pay by relinquishing some of our privacy. Social media advertising is lucrative because it is tailored to each user, based on detailed profiles of the user's online reading and purchasing habits. And we pay through higher prices on the products and services that are advertised. To the extent they can, advertisers recoup their advertising expenses by passing them on to consumers in the form of higher prices.

Finally, the content identification systems used by YouTube, Facebook, and other social media sites sweep many false positives in their net. In addition to simply misidentifying music and videos as potentially infringing, the systems do not readily distinguish between user postings that infringe copyright and those that qualify as fair use. As a result, some small percentage of fair use and otherwise noninfringing postings are removed. And even for the vast majority of such postings that remain online, the content identification systems effectively enable copyright owners to monetize—for themselves—many postings that copy their work in ways that qualify as fair use. Users who have created such fair use postings might want to reap the advertising revenue generated by their postings themselves rather than seeing the revenue flow to the owner of the copyright in the copied content. Further, especially if a user's fair use video is critical of a copyrighted work or copyright owner, the user might adamantly oppose having the video used to generate advertising revenue for the object of the user's criticism—or might not want advertisements generated alongside the video at all. Under copyright law, a person who makes a fair use of someone else's work in creating a new work is entitled to copyright in that new work (at least insofar as the new work reflects its creator's own creative contribution). But if you post your fair use video on a social media site, copyright law does not require that site to obtain your permission for its placement of advertising alongside your video or for how it allocates revenue from that advertising.

It is difficult to weigh those costs of advertising against the benefits of enabling copyright owners (and social media platforms) to earn revenue from social media file sharing while keeping the vast majority of user-posted videos online for others to enjoy. There are some significant advantages to a system, such as that in effect for YouTube, in which advertising makes it possible for the vast majority of user-posted videos containing copyrighted content to remain online. But it is not a panacea.

Should copyright law make it illegal to circumvent technologies that copyright holders use to control access to copyrighted expression?

In the late 1990s, the motion picture studios and record labels implemented a technological solution to the threat of massive illicit file sharing. They began to encode digital copies of movies and recorded music with software designed to prevent unauthorized copying of and access to those works. For example, the major movie studios used software encryption known as Content Scramble System (CSS) on DVDs of their movies. CSS prevents ripping and copying the movie from the DVD. In addition, only DVD players that contain a proprietary software key that decrypts CSS can play CSS-encrypted DVDs. CSS and other such software tools are commonly called "technological protection measures" or "digital rights management."

The industries realized, however, that any technological measures that were simple and inexpensive enough to affix to mass-produced CDs or DVDs would soon be hacked and circumvented. Indeed, CSS was defeated within a couple years of its introduction by a widely disseminated de-encryption program labeled DeCSS. The studios and labels accordingly lobbied Congress to amend the Copyright Act to make it illegal to circumvent technological protection measures or to distribute software or other devices designed to enable consumers to circumvent.

When Congress enacted the Digital Millennium Copyright Act of 1998 (DMCA) it codified a compromise between the copyright and telecommunications industries. To encourage copyright industries to make their content available in digital formats, Congress enacted anti-circumvention provisions sponsored by the copyright industry. But to give the telecommunications industries sufficient legal certainty for them to invest in building the Internet and providing online services, Congress enacted the Internet service provider safe harbors that I have discussed.

The DMCA outlaws circumventing technological measures that control access to copyrighted works. It also forbids distributing software or devices that may be used to circumvent technological access or copying controls. Notably, then, the DMCA anti-circumvention provisions do not merely outlaw circumventing those technological measures that are designed to prevent illicit copying. They also protect technological measures that control *access* to copyrighted works—even if gaining access does not involve copying. One leading case held, for example, that it is illegal to distribute DeCSS to users of the open source Linux operating system so they can watch movies on CSS-encrypted DVDs on their personal computer.

In effect, therefore, the DMCA gave copyright holders a right that never before existed: the right to control access to works in digital format. In principle, copyright holders could use that right to charge for each and every use of a copyrighted work, essentially to rent the work for specific times or uses rather than selling copies. DMCA opponents decried the ensuing specter of a "pay-per-use society." The copyright industries responded that the ability to charge for access and use would make it possible for them to better serve consumers. It would enable them to offer a menu of different options and pricing. A consumer who wishes to download a copy of a movie would pay more than a consumer who merely views the movie once or rents it for a limited period of time.

As the home entertainment marketplace has developed, it appears that the copyright industries have the better argument. Granted, consumers prefer buying physical media and media players that are free from technological protection measures. But the home entertainment market is rapidly moving from physical media to online streaming. And streaming services rely on technological protection measures to stream content only to those who register for their service.

Technological protection measures also enable streaming services to charge differential pricing for different services. They make it possible, for example, for iTunes and Amazon to charge a lower price for "renting" a movie for twenty-four hours than for purchasing a copy for permanent download. They also enable Pandora, Spotify, and Apple Music to offer premium music streaming services at a far lower price per song streamed than iTunes's sales of songs for download.

In sum, the problem with the DMCA anti-circumvention provisions is not with the concept of pay-per-use in and of itself. Indeed, streaming services secured by technological protections are now rapidly overtaking selling copies or downloads as consumers' preferred method of viewing and listening to movies, TV shows, and music on their computers and mobile devices.

Rather, the anti-circumvention provisions are cause for concern because they lack the exceptions and limitations that apply to traditional copyright rights. Notably, as interpreted by several courts, the anti-circumvention prohibitions apply even if an individual seeks to gain access in order to engage in noninfringing fair use. For example, a reporter who circumvented the technological protection on a CD containing internal corporate communications in order to uncover damning evidence of the corporation's misdeeds would violate the anti-circumvention provisions—as would the purveyor of the software that the reporter uses to circumvent—even though the reporter's copying of the communications would likely qualify as fair use.

Does the Copyright Office's triennial rulemaking authorize individuals to circumvent access controls to engage in fair use?

Sometimes. But, overall, the triennial rulemaking provides grossly inadequate protection for fair use.

In order to mitigate the potentially harsh effects of the DMCA anti-circumvention prohibitions, Congress directed the Copyright Office to engage in a triennial rulemaking proceeding to recommend that the Librarian of Congress issue three-year exemptions from the anti-circumvention prohibition as needed to enable "noninfringing uses . . . of a particular class of copyrighted works." In 2015, for example, the Librarian of Congress granted a three-year exemption to those who circumvent technological measures on DVDs containing movies and television shows in order to make noncommercial remix videos, use footage in documentary films, or for classroom education purposes.

Nonetheless, the triennial rulemaking fails adequately to protect fair use in three fundamental ways. First, the Librarian of Congress' exemptions last only three years. Those who want a continued exemption from the anti-circumvention prohibition must apply every three years. In June 2017, the Copyright Office established a streamlined procedure for applying to renew an exemption. But the renewal applicant must submit evidence that an exemption is still needed to engage in noninfringing uses in light of changing marketplace conditions.

Second, under the DMCA, the Librarian of Congress can only exempt the actual act of circumventing; it has no power to provide exemptions for distributing the software or other tools that most people need in order to circumvent. As a result, it remains illegal to distribute DeCSS or other de-encryption tools that amateur remixers, documentary filmmakers, and educators need to take advantage of the 2015 exemption for circumventing DVD controls to engage in certain fair uses of movies and TV shows.

Third, the Librarian provides exemptions only for particular classes of copyright works that must be accessed to engage in noninfringing uses, particular media in which those works are embodied, and particular infringing uses for which the works need to be accessed. As noted above, for example, the 2015 rulemaking exempts circumventing CSS on DVDs in order to make certain specified uses of movies and TV shows embodied on the DVD. As such, the triennial rulemaking is too blunt an instrument to adequately protect fair use. Fair use requires an individualized determination of each particular use. It is not limited to specified works, media, or uses.

In its 2015 rulemaking, for example, the Librarian of Congress declined to exempt circumvention to copy short clips of existing movies and television shows for the purpose of including such clips in fictional, as opposed to documentary, films. In so doing, the Librarian adopted the Copyright Office's finding that copying another's work in a fictional film, the purpose of which is typically for entertainment, is unlikely to be a fair use. The Copyright Office is not entirely wrong. In general, copying a clip for a fictional film is probably less likely to be fair use than doing so for a documentary film. But fair use requires an individualized determination, not a general, across-the-board rule. And courts have repeatedly held that copying from another work for inclusion in a fictional film or television show may constitute fair use in particular cases, depending on the facts of each case. Nonetheless, the DMCA anti-circumvention provisions make it illegal to circumvent CSS for the purpose of copying a clip for a fictional film even when that act of copying qualifies as fair use.

Should unlicensed remixes infringe copyright?

Artists and authors have borrowed from earlier works for as long as can be remembered. But digital technology greatly enhances the ease with which we can copy and remix portions of preexisting works to create a new creative work. Some remixes consist entirely of parts of preexisting songs, videos, or texts that are edited, altered, and combined to appear as one. Others deploy digital sampling, a technique for incorporating lines or riffs from existing sound recordings with newly recorded music. Some remixes are created by fans of a particular work or TV series to reinterpret or build on elements of that work. Others incorporate elements of sundry preexisting works to make an unrelated or loosely related artistic or political statement. There are almost infinite ways in which remixers use, meld, manipulate, and juxtapose disparate portions of existing works to create new expression—and such remixes have come to be a ubiquitous part of the social media landscape.

Larry Lessig famously coined the term "remix culture" to connote the widespread practice of using existing cultural expression as raw material for creating new creative expression, primarily, although not entirely, through digital technology.

Yet not everyone celebrates remix culture. Many copyright holders and authors vociferously object to what they regard as the mining of their work without permission or compensation. Some judges share that view. As noted above, one ruling holding that digital sampling constitutes copyright infringement began with the biblical injunction: "Thou shalt not steal."

Instances of conflict between remix culture and copyright holders abound. One seminal example is *The Grey Album*, a critically acclaimed mashup album produced and released in 2004 by a musician and record producer known by his stage name, Danger Mouse. Danger Mouse took an a cappella version of rapper Jay-Z's *Black Album* and coupled it with instrumentals that he digitally created from samples taken from The Beatles's *White Album*. The resulting *The Grey Album* catapulted to fame when EMI—the owner of the copyright in the Beatles's sound recording—tried to block the mashup's distribution despite Jay-Z's, Paul McCartney's, and Ringo Starr's approval of the project. EMI's attempt sparked a day of coordinated civil disobedience, termed "Grey Tuesday," in which roughly 170 websites offered the mashup album for free download, resulting in over 100,000 copies downloaded on that day alone.

At this point, the major motion picture studios, book publishers, and record labels seem largely to have acquiesced in amateur remixes, such as YouTube videos and fan creations— so long as the remixes remain noncommercial. Notably, CBS Studios and Paramount Pictures, the joint holders of the copyrights in *Star Trek*, recently issued "guidelines" for creators of *Star Trek* fan productions who wish to avoid getting hit with a copyright infringement lawsuit. The guidelines state that CBS and Paramount "are big believers in reasonable fan fiction and fan creativity, and, in particular, want amateur fan filmmakers to showcase their passion for *Star Trek*." To avoid possible legal action, the guidelines require, among other things, that the productions be noncommercial, entirely amateur, and, at most, fifteen minutes long.

By contrast, some authors insist that even amateur remixes are parasitic on existing work and thus not truly creative. For them, any borrowing from someone else's creative work should require permission. And copyright law should properly serve to compel would-be authors to be "truly creative" by producing works that are entirely original rather than attempting to free ride off of someone else's creative product.

That view presents an inaccurate portrait of artistic creativity. Virtually all great art, music, literature, and film copies from earlier work. Shakespeare plundered the plots of Ovid, Plautus, Boccaccio, Cinthio, and Christopher Marlowe. Picasso brazenly appropriated from Delacroix, Velazquez, and Manet. Beethoven reworked Diabell; Liszt took from Mozart; Dvorak regularly employed themes from Moravian and Bohemian folk music; and Handel transformatively plagiarized from numerous sources. Modern composers have created Broadway musical versions of Shakespeare's *Romeo and Juliet*, Victor Hugo's *Les Misérables*, Voltaire's *Candide*, L. Frank Baum's *The Wonderful Wizard of Oz*, and Harold Gray's *Annie* comic strip. Disney has produced animated versions of numerous folk tales, as well as creative reworkings of fairy tales authored by Hans Christian Anderson, Charles Perrault, and the Brothers Grimm.

At one time, copyright law fully comported with this venerable artistic practice of reworking existing material. Throughout most of the nineteenth century, authors had an exclusive right to print their work but not to prevent creative transformations, translations, or fair abridgements, so long as the reworking did not supplant demand for the original. But copyright's scope has dramatically expanded since the late nineteenth century. Today's remixes typically infringe the copyright holder's exclusive right to create derivative works unless excused as fair use.

As discussed in Chapter IV, recent rulings suggest that using an existing work as raw material for substantially new and original creative expression will qualify as fair use even

if the remix was not created for a fundamentally different expressive purpose, like parody or biography. Those rulings
throw open fair use doctrine to some uncertainty and un-
predictability. But from a copyright policy perspective they
make a great deal of sense. In a roundabout way, they bring
copyright law back into harmony with the nature of human
creativity. Remixes should not infringe copyright unless they
substitute for the original work or undermine investment in
capital-intensive derivative works like Hollywood sequels of
full-length feature films.

I bought it. Don't I own it? Should consumers be allowed to copy their music and movies onto multiple devices and cloud storage?

Consumers want to access their music, videos, ebooks, and
images from multiple devices. To do that, they might want to
make multiple copies of those works, whether for back-up or
accessing on multiple devices offline. They might also want
to upload content from their computers onto cloud storage
platforms, like Google Drive and Dropbox, for accessing it
anywhere and anytime via the Internet or a mobile data network. Does copyright law permit such copying? Should it?

It is pretty clear that downloading copyrighted works from
illicit file-trading networks is infringing—and making multiple copies of those infringing files would also infringe copyright. But what about copies that consumers have purchased
or that, like recordings of TV shows for later viewing, are fair
use copies?

The copyright industries' position is that, at least in principle, any copying, even of purchased content, is infringing.
Jack Valenti, former president of the MPAA, put it crisply: "If
you buy a DVD, you have a copy. If you want a backup copy,
you buy another one."[16] As noted in Chapter IV, however, lower
courts have suggested that "space-shifting"—reproducing a
purchased copy housed on one device and saving the copy

on another—is a noninfringing "paradigmatic noncommercial personal use."

Further, copyright industry spokespersons have stated that such copying is a "tolerated use" for the time being. The industries sometimes try to make such copying more difficult by suing providers of services that consumers use to space-shift. For example, studios sued Dish Networks over its Hopper service, which enables consumers to view recorded program from multiple devices. Copyright holders also obstruct copying by applying technological protection measures to their content. However, they apparently have no plans to sue consumers who engage in space-shifting.

In the meantime, in its 2014 ruling in *American Broadcasting Companies v. Aereo*, the Supreme Court put off for another day the question of whether providing cloud services through which consumers store and access copyrighted content requires copyright holders' permission. But so long as cloud storage consumers are truly using the service for personal use, not to share publicly, it seems likely that no copyright owner permission is required.

As I have discussed, there are some benefits to empowering copyright holders to control when users can and cannot copy copyrighted content. That control enables copyright holders to charge different prices for renting, downloading, and streaming content, thus giving consumers a greater menu of choices than merely having to pay to own a permanent copy. Arguably, the same rationale could apply to space-shifting. Consumers could pay the highest price for a copy that comes with the right to make and store additional copies for playback on multiple devices and a far lower price for a copy that is tethered to a single device.

Such a regime would most probably run up against the overwhelming weight of consumer expectations, however. We are used to the distinction between renting, paying for a one-time experience, and purchasing. But once we have purchased an item, we feel that it is our prerogative to consume it at our convenience in the privacy of our home, car, or office. And with today's technology, that means accessing our content from multiple devices. Hence, despite some copyright industry ruminations to the contrary, there seems to be a broad consensus that consumers should be entitled to copy on multiple devices or in cloud storage any music, videos, or other works that they have lawfully made or acquired, as well as to stream that content to themselves.

Does the supplier of a product that many people use to infringe copyright face liability for those users' infringements when the product also has noninfringing uses?

Many products are multiple-use devices. In other words, they can be used for both infringing and noninfringing purposes. I can use a photocopier to make photocopies of a public domain text or a short passage of a book for teaching purposes. Those uses are both noninfringing. But I can use the same photocopier to produce for sale 1,000 copies of a best-selling novel. That use is clearly infringing. Likewise, I can use peer-to-peer file-trading software to gain an audience for my own songs (not infringing) or to distribute my collection of Beatles' recordings to 10 million of my closest friends (obviously infringing).

Under longstanding copyright doctrine, if Sam knowingly provides Reuben with a device or other means for Reuben to infringe, Sam is contributorily liable for Reuben's infringement. Suppliers of multiple-use devices obviously know that some people will use their devices to infringe. Does that mean that the supplier of a multiple-use device or software platform is contributorily liable for users' copyright infringements?

That question has significant ramifications for copyright holders as well as for producers and suppliers of devices that consumers use to share cultural works. After all, virtually every device that we use to communicate with one another—from smart phones to PCs—is capable of copying and distributing copyrighted expression. If suppliers of products—say, peer-to-peer file-trading software—used for copyright infringement on a massive, global scale face no liability, copyright holders will often be left with no effective means to enforce their copyrights. But if device suppliers do face liability merely because their device is capable of being used to infringe, that will pose a significant barrier to consumer-friendly technological innovation.

The short answer to the question of supplier liability is that, in general, suppliers of multiple-use consumer goods are not liable for user infringements unless the supplier has actively encouraged purchasers to infringe. The two leading cases are *Sony Corp. v. Universal City Studios*, which the Supreme Court decided in 1984, and *MGM v. Grokster*, which the Supreme Court decided in 2005.

Sony Corp. v. Universal City Studios is often referred to as the "Betamax case." In the early 1980s, Sony's Betamax video tape recorder was used by millions of American to record television programs. Two leading television studios—Universal Pictures and Walt Disney Productions—sued Sony, along with some retail establishments that sold the Betamax, on the theory that they were liable for Betamax users' copyright infringements. The Supreme Court held in favor of Sony and the retailers. It reasoned that a supplier of a "staple article of commerce"— meaning a mass-produced consumer good, as opposed to a custom-made good—that is capable of substantial noninfringing uses is not liable for infringing uses of the article, even if the supplier must know that some people use the article to infringe. The Court referred to this rule as the "staple article of commerce doctrine." The Court then held that recording a television program for later viewing is fair use—and thus that the vast majority of uses of the Betamax were not infringing. Given that substantial noninfringing use, Sony and the retailers were not contributorily liable for any uses of the Betamax that did infringe.

In reaching its holding, the *Sony* Court emphasized the need to maintain copyright law's delicate balance between providing an incentive for the creation of original expression and allowing for the development of new technologies. The Court noted that Congress has repeatedly enacted Copyright Act amendments to address that balance with respect to new technologies (primarily through statutory licensing). It further stated that "[t]he staple article of commerce doctrine must strike a balance between a copyright holder's legitimate demand for effective—not merely symbolic—protection of the statutory monopoly, and the rights of others freely to engage in substantially unrelated areas of commerce."

In *MGM v. Grokster*, the Supreme Court had the occasion to revisit its ruling in *Sony*. Grokster and its co-defendants were purveyors of peer-to-peer file-trading software. They argued successfully before the district court and appellate court that they were not contributorily liable for individuals' use of their software to infringe the plaintiff motion picture studios' copyrights. The lower courts applied *Sony*, which they read as holding that the distribution of a commercial product capable of substantial noninfringing uses does not give rise to contributory liability for infringement unless the distributor knows of specific instances of infringement and fails to act on that knowledge to prevent the infringement. The district court further found that up to 10 percent of files traded using the defendants' software was not infringing, primarily because some aspiring musicians and recording artists gave consent to have their songs shared. For the district court and Ninth Circuit Court of Appeals, that was sufficient to support a finding that the software was "capable of substantial noninfringing uses."

The lower court rulings were also premised on the finding that Grokster and its co-defendants had no actual knowledge of specific infringements. It was only the users who searched for, retrieved, and stored the infringing files. The defendants had no involvement beyond providing the software in the first place.

The Supreme Court reversed. It held that the staple article of commerce doctrine set out by *Sony* is not the only possible ground for contributory liability. Rather, the Supreme Court held in *Grokster* that one who distributes a multiple-use device with the purpose of promoting copyright infringement and who takes clear, affirmative steps to foster such infringement is liable for any resulting infringing uses. Grokster had acted to induce infringement when it advertised itself as the new Napster, a pioneering peer-to-peer service that courts had previously shut down for contributory copyright infringement.

In principle, going forward from *Grokster*, it should be relatively easy for a supplier of a multiple-use device to avoid liability for users' infringements. The supplier and its personnel need merely avoid making any statements, whether in advertising or internal communications, that show an intention to distribute the device to foster infringement. Absent such damning statements in the record, the far more solicitous standard set out in *Sony* will apply.

Importantly, however, *Sony* does not govern claims of liability levied against suppliers of ongoing *services* rather than staple articles of commerce. Copyright doctrine distinguishes between suppliers of a good, who typically have no control over how consumers use it, and suppliers of a service or website platform, who maintain an ongoing relationship with the user and thus have greater responsibility to prevent infringement. Accordingly, YouTube, Facebook, and other providers of user-generated content platforms cannot avail themselves of *Sony*. For that reason, prior to enactment of the DMCA safe harbor for Internet service providers in 1998, Internet service providers faced potential liability for their subscribers' infringements. Today, they must typically rely on the DMCA safe harbor to avoid copyright infringement liability.

Should YouTube, Facebook, and other social media platforms be liable for their users' infringements?

In Viacom's billion-dollar copyright infringement lawsuit against YouTube, Viacom presented evidence that YouTube's founders built their business on hosting thousands of infringing clips of popular movies and TV programs posted by YouTube subscribers. By contrast, Google (which acquired YouTube about twenty months after the user-generated content site was founded) argued that it would have been impossible for the YouTube founders to identify which clips were infringing and which were not. In support, Google introduced evidence that Viacom had surreptitiously uploaded clips of its own movies and TV programs onto YouTube using fictitious user names in order to promote Viacom content without revealing that Viacom itself was behind that promotion. In addition, in the early days of YouTube, like today, numerous user videos combined portions of copyright-protected video or music with the user's own original expression. It was thus far from obvious which of those videos were infringing and which might qualify as fair use.

As noted in Chapter II, Viacom's lawsuit ended in an overwhelming victory for Google based on the court's reading of the DMCA safe harbor for Internet intermediaries. Like other judicial rulings regarding the safe harbor, the U.S. Court of Appeals for the Second Circuit held in the YouTube case that an Internet intermediary typically enjoys the benefit of the safe harbor unless it has actual knowledge of specific infringements on its system (or deliberately avoids gaining that knowledge) and fails to remove the infringing material expeditiously. Having just general knowledge that there is a lot of infringement is not enough to disqualify the intermediary from the safe harbor. With that and a couple other narrow exceptions, the courts have ruled that Internet intermediaries face no liability for infringements on their system so long as they respond expeditiously to copyright owner takedown notices—which must identify the online location and identity of specific infringing copies—and have a reasonable policy of terminating service to repeat infringers. An Internet intermediary has no duty to police for infringement or to proactively filter out infringing material, even if it is generally aware that a great deal of infringing content resides on its system.

In response, copyright industries and various authors' trade associations argue that the DMCA safe harbor, as the courts have interpreted it, tilts too far toward exonerating Internet intermediaries who profit from massive copyright infringement. They insist that existing law puts an onerous, unfair burden on the copyright owner. Copyright owners must continually police the Internet for infringing material. And copyright owners face a "whack-a-mole" problem: for every infringing copy that Internet intermediaries take down in response to a copyright owner takedown notice, another infringing copy of the same work quickly takes its place— posted by the same user or someone else. The result is that social media sites and search engines remain conduits for massive amounts of infringing content. Copyright industries and authors argue, indeed, that the safe harbor provision "as construed by the courts incentivizes scrupulous inattention and inactivity by service providers to mass infringement they know to be occurring through their sites and services, and provides protection for bad actors who build businesses based on copyright infringement."[17]

The copyright industries and authors' associations offer various proposals for modifying the DMCA safe harbor. At the very least, they contend, the safe harbor should be conditional on "takedown and stay down." Once notified of an infringing user-posted copy of a particular movie, TV show, or music recording, Internet intermediaries should bear the burden of locating and promptly removing any reposting of that copyright-protected work by any user.

Further, the copyright industries and authors insist that Internet intermediaries should face copyright infringement liability for failing to proactively prevent infringing material from being uploaded in the first instance. In other words, intermediaries should be required to implement filtering systems that automatically identify and block postings of infringing materials by comparing digital information in user-posted content with metadata for copyrighted works that copyright owners supply. In addition, copyright owners object that courts have interpreted the safe harbor to extend to intermediaries that do far more than merely host user content. They argue that the safe harbor should not be available for intermediaries, like YouTube, that display thumbnails of other videos on the platform "related" to the video the user is viewing, recommend videos based on a user's prior viewing history, and enable users to search for videos by keyword.

Should Congress answer the call to narrow the safe harbor? Should it amend the Copyright Act to put a greater onus on Internet intermediaries to police for infringement? The problem with such proposals is that they would greatly burden new Internet platforms and social media, with costs to both technological innovation and expressive diversity.

YouTube provides an apt example. At its inception, YouTube knowingly benefited from the availability on its site of infringing video clips of popular TV shows and movies to attract many new users. But if YouTube had faced the burden of active policing or of crushing copyright infringement liability from the get-go, it might never have gotten off the ground. And even if YouTube had survived, it would have faced incentives to over-police—to remove any material that poses any risk of potential infringement—in order to avoid liability, resulting in far fewer user-posted remixes, mash-ups, and creative montages of existing expression. Either way, YouTube would never have grown to what it is today: a vital source of user-generated entertainment, social commentary, and news reporting from all over the world. YouTube has also become a platform of choice for traditional copyright industries, which both upload their own original content and receive royalties for user posts of copyrighted material, pursuant to licensing agreements with YouTube. What's more, as YouTube has grown and established lucrative licensing arrangements with copyright holders, it has voluntarily implemented costly systems to enable copyright owners to reduce—or monetize—user infringements on its site. Facebook and other established Internet intermediaries have instituted similar systems.

Of course, unlike YouTube, some user-posted content and streaming platforms are wholly dedicated to profiting off infringing material. Yet those pirate sites are mostly based outside the United States. Recalibrating the Internet service provider safe harbor under U.S. copyright law would have minimal impact on them.

In any event, copyright law should not give incumbent copyright industries the power to stifle competition from Internet platforms and new media in the market for online content aggregation and distribution. Imposing liability on social media for failing to discover and root out infringing material on their systems would risk giving incumbent copyright industries that power.

Should social media be required to deploy digital technologies to filter out infringing material?

Copyright industries demand that social media sites that host user-posted content be required to implement filtering systems like Audible Magic's automated content recognition system and YouTube's Content ID as a condition to enjoy the DMCA safe harbor. That demand should be rejected. To require that social media sites deploy filtering systems would impose a costly burden on new Internet platforms, most of which lack the immense resources of Google and Facebook. It could also lead to the suppression of considerable noninfringing expression.

Filtering systems are expensive to implement. Further, since no filtering system is 100 percent effective, a legal requirement to filter would likely pose difficult cases involving just how effective the filtering must be to meet the requirement. It would thus leave social media sites with the risk of liability for failure to filter adequately. In turn, like in any business on which a change in the law imposes additional costs and risk of liability, requiring filtering would result in a reduction of investment in user-generated content platforms and other social media. Indeed, to the extent that platforms like the early YouTube depend upon the ready availability of popular copyrighted works to get off the ground, filtering requirements would be a deterrent to entry into the market for social media.

In short, filtering systems are best left to voluntary implementation by mature Internet intermediaries, like Facebook and Google's YouTube. Such mature intermediaries have a strong incentive to implement automated content identification systems that enable rights holders to monetize user postings of copyrighted content through sharing advertising revenues with the Internet intermediary. YouTube already pays music rights holders over $1 billion a year in licensing revenues and, undoubtedly, earns much more from its share of advertising revenues generated by user postings of copyrighted recorded music. However, while mature Internet intermediaries have the wherewithal and incentive to implement content identification systems and related licensing arrangements with rights holders, if copyright law imposed content identification and filtering requirements, that would unduly burden new social media platforms and impede technological innovation.

Moreover, even for YouTube and other well-heeled Internet platforms, the problem remains that filtering sweeps considerable noninfringing user-posted content into its net. YouTube's Content ID system tags user-posted videos that match metadata supplied by copyright owners. The system seems to work well much of time. But it also generates some disturbing false positives. In the summer of 2012, for example, YouTube's filter erroneously took down the official live stream of the Democratic National Convention, replacing it with a notice over a black screen indicating that the blocked video contained content from Associated Press, Dow Jones, New York Times Digital, and several other copyright holders, "one or more of whom have blocked it in your country on copyright grounds."

More generally, YouTube's Content ID system cannot readily distinguish infringing video clips from video remixes, mash-ups, commentary, and fan fiction sequels that are probably fair use. Content ID regularly tags noninfringing videos, and YouTube leaves it to the copyright owner to determine how to proceed whenever a video is tagged. Educational videos about popular culture and videos with the same or similar name as a copyright work also fall victim to a filtering system based on copyright owner–supplied metadata.

As noted above, when YouTube's Content ID tags a noninfringing user-posted video, the user-posted video is rarely removed from YouTube. Copyright owners almost always choose to monetize user videos tagged by Content ID rather than remove them. Some users might object to the exploitation of their fair use or otherwise noninfringing video to generate revenue for a copyright owner. But at least the user-posted video remains on YouTube for all to see. Moreover, YouTube provides a right of appeal to users whose videos have been flagged.

However, the copyright owner's decision to monetize rather than remove a user-posted YouTube video is a voluntary choice, not a legal requirement. Nor does the law require YouTube to provide its users with a right of appeal. If the DMCA were amended to require that user-posted content platforms implement filtering as a condition to enjoying the safe harbor, there is no guarantee that erroneously tagged noninfringing speech would generally remain online.

Removing noninfringing user-posted content has profound implications. Copyright law imposes limitations and exceptions on copyright holder rights, including fair use and copyright's limited duration, to ensure that copyrights do not unduly suppress free speech and authors' ability to creatively build on the work of their predecessors. Online enforcement by automated filtering systems could radically alter that balance. It would threaten to run roughshod over fair use and other copyright limitations in the very user-generated content and social media platforms that serve as a vital wellspring for user creativity and expressive diversity in our age.[18]

Today, neither copyright law nor the First Amendment prevent social media platforms and copyright owners from implementing such private ordering through contract and automated enforcement. To prevent that deleterious result, Congress should amend the Copyright Act to provide users with a statutory right to appeal the filtering of content they have posted—much as YouTube voluntarily provides for its users whose videos have been flagged by Content ID as infringing. The Copyright Act should require automated content identification systems to incorporate a speedy, user-friendly mechanism under which the Internet platform must undo the filtering of content that a user asserts is, in fact, not infringing. In such cases, if the copyright owner still insists that the content is infringing, the dispute should be resolved in court. Without that user protection, automated filtering could too often block music and videos that are mistakenly identified as infringing, including fair use, false positive identifications, and postings of works that are in the public domain.

Should statutory and other compulsory licenses be expanded or contracted in the digital arena?

As we have seen, several copyright licensing markets operate under statutory or judicially imposed compulsory licenses. These licenses entitle the copyright owner to receive reasonable compensation for particular types of uses of copyrighted works, while denying the copyright owner the right to prohibit such uses. Congress has typically enacted compulsory licenses as a compromise solution to battles between copyright industries and new media distributors of copyrighted works. Such new media distributors include record labels (when sound recordings were new media in the early twentieth century), cable and satellite television, radio, digital home recording of music, digital downloads, and webcasting.

Should the compulsory licensing model be extended to more digital media and uses of copyrighted expression? Or, by contrast, does digital technology render compulsory licensing less necessary—and less justifiable—than previously? Those questions stand at the heart of several current copyright battles.

I provide some tentative answers in the next question. Here we consider three underlying issues coloring the debate over compulsory licensing.

First, are compulsory licenses discrete, disfavored exceptions to the general rule that copyrights are exclusive proprietary rights? Or are compulsory licenses a central feature of copyright law?

A number of commentators and copyright industry stakeholders insist that compulsory licenses are narrow, disfavored exceptions to copyright holders' exclusive rights. So has the Copyright Office and some courts. In their view, copyright holders should normally have the prerogative to grant copyright licenses only on terms with which the copyright holder voluntarily agrees. Compulsory licenses are needed only to address specific instances of market failure (where voluntary bargaining is highly impractical) and should remain in force only so long as the market failure persists.

By contrast, other commentators view statutory and judicially imposed compulsory licenses as a central feature of copyright law that should be applied more broadly. For them, compulsory licensing is often the best arrangement for providing an adequate incentive for the creation of original expression, while also spurring technological innovation in the distribution, organization, and consumption of that expression. They also note that the Copyright Act typically provides affected industries with an opportunity to reach voluntary agreement, albeit under the shadow of a statutory license, before a panel of Copyright Royalty Judges steps in to determine the statutory license rate.

Those contrasting positions reflect philosophical differences regarding the nature of copyright and the efficacy of voluntary copyright licensing markets. Those who believe that authors have a natural property right in their creations and/or that markets function quite well in making copyrighted works available to the public typically oppose compulsory licensing except in the most narrow of circumstances. By contrast, those who favor compulsory licenses tend to view copyright as a limited government grant that should be narrowly tailored to serve the public good. They also contend that incumbent copyright industries have strong incentives to deploy exclusive, proprietary rights to stifle disruptive innovation and suppress competition in the market for disseminating cultural works.

Second, the debate over compulsory licensing rests on different assumptions about the promise of digital technology. Opponents of compulsory licensing believe that digital technology facilitates an efficient market for voluntary copyright licenses. They trumpet digital systems that make it possible to identify and track uses, automatically charge consumers for their uses, and embed information regarding copyright ownership and licensing terms within digital copies produced by the copyright owner. Those technologies, they maintain, present unprecedented opportunities to minimize licensing transaction costs and to enable copyright owners to charge different prices for different uses depending on how much the consumer values the use. In short, they believe that digital licensing and rights management systems can underwrite a highly efficient, welfare-enhancing copyright market, thus avoiding the need for compulsory licensing.

By contrast, those who champion compulsory licensing have little faith that digital licensing and rights management systems would truly serve consumer demand and the public interest. They fear that, with or without digital licensing, exclusive rights present a major obstacle to establishing the near universal, publicly accessible libraries of books, sound recordings, films, and images that consumers and the public interest demand. Copyright holders who hold enforceable exclusive rights will be unwilling to grant permission to include their entire repertoire in new media platforms that aspire to provide access to all works of a given type. Indeed, compulsory license proponents hold that in a purely proprietary copyright system even major studios, labels, and publishers lack the capacity to license universal libraries since those copyright industries often do not own all of the relevant copyrights they need to license a given work. Further, compulsory licensing proponents maintain that digital control and licensing systems that enable tracking and charging for each use would dampen the freewheeling culture of remixing, quoting, reposting, reformulating, and discussing existing works that defines social media today. At bottom, those who favor expanding compulsory licensing insist that incumbent copyright industries consistently use exclusive rights under copyright law to erect fortifications around their own dominant positions, proprietary platforms, and business models—and that minimizing licensing transaction costs would not alter that practice.

Third, industry stakeholders naturally take positions in the debate that reflect whether they benefit from the particular compulsory license regime in question. Record labels have traditionally championed the compulsory license for cover recordings, which enables them to pay the below-market statutory rate to songwriters of previously recorded songs that the label wishes to rerecord. But the labels would much prefer market bargaining and voluntary licensing, rather than the current statutory license, for the webcasters' streaming of the labels' sound recordings.

Recently, the Recording Industry Association of America called for an extended blanket license, presumably backed by the Copyright Act and antitrust exemptions, whereby organizations representing all songwriters, music publishers, and record labels would enter into a binding agreement on how to divide royalties paid by users. According to this proposal, even if compulsory licensing remains in place, compulsory license rates would mimic market bargaining. The rates would be determined in accordance with hypothetical willing seller/

willing buyer rates—a rate that is more favorable to copyright owners than most compulsory license rates today.

For their part, the large music publishers wish to partly withdraw their vast repertoires of copyrighted songs from ASCAP so they can negotiate licenses with online music streaming services free of the ASCAP antitrust consent decree. The streaming services, by contrast, favor universal compulsory licenses for musical compositions and sound recordings instead of having to negotiate licenses with record labels for permission to provide "interactive services"—those that enable consumers to select which songs they wish to hear—as is the case under current copyright law.

Which is the better view regarding compulsory licensing in the digital era?

There is much about the patchwork of compulsory licenses and the proceedings for determining statutory rates that could be improved. For example, there is currently no mechanism whereby a digital download service like iTunes can obtain a blanket statutory license for all recorded songs. Rather, the compulsory license for digital downloads requires that iTunes must pay musical work copyright owners on a per song, per digital download basis. In addition, the Apple Music streaming service enjoys the benefit of the compulsory license that the antitrust decree imposes on ASCAP and BMI for streaming musical compositions but must obtain permission from the record labels to stream the sound recordings featuring performed renditions of the compositions.

Further, when Pandora streams recorded music on its Internet radio stations, it must pay statutory license rates based on the willing seller/willing buyer rate for streaming the sound recordings. As set by the Copyright Royalty Judges, that rate is currently 0.17 cents per song streamed, which amounts to some 50 percent of Pandora's revenue. Yet, for streaming musical compositions, Pandora pays to songwriters and music publishers considerably lower rates. Those rates are set by the courts that preside, respectively, over the ASCAP and BMI antitrust consent decrees, courts that the consent decrees label the "rate courts." Nor are the ASCAP and BMI rates the same. The ASCAP rate court ordered that Pandora pay ASCAP a 1.85-percent royalty rate, while the BMI rate court ordered that Pandora pay BMI a 2.5-percent royalty rate. According to both rulings, those rates are supposed to reflect what a willing buyer would pay a willing seller in a competitive market—a market that is hypothetical given that ASCAP and BMI have monopolies in the market for music performance licenses. But ASCAP and BMI each bear the burden of proving to their respective rate court that their proposed rates are reasonable. (More recently, Pandora reached a settlement with ASCAP and BMI under which it will pay royalties at undisclosed rates.)

In addition, under the Copyright Act, the statutory license that applies to satellite radio transmissions of sound recordings imposes the more licensee friendly fair income/ fair return standard, not the willing seller/willing buyer rate. What's more, terrestrial radio stations pay nothing for broadcasting sound recordings and, per rate court rulings, only a 1.7-percent royalty rate for broadcasting and streaming musical compositions.

Finally, while the Copyright Act's statutory license provisions for webcasting, cable retransmissions, and other uses typically aim to encourage industry-wide negotiated agreements, the industries repeatedly fail to reach agreement. As a result, they end up in complex, highly costly rate proceedings before administrative judges, sometimes followed by litigation and lobbying Congress for rate adjustments.

These inconsistencies and administrative burdens suggest the need to reform copyright's various compulsory licensing regimes. But that is not to say that compulsory licenses should be jettisoned. Indeed, compulsory licenses must be seen as a critical tool for achieving copyright's fundamental purposes, not an anomalous, disfavored exception to exclusive copyright holder rights. Compulsory licenses will sometimes be superior to exclusive rights in two principal respects.

First, compulsory licensing advocates are correct: a proprietary copyright regime cannot deliver on one of digital technology's great promises: the creation of searchable universal libraries of substantially all music, writings, films, television shows, and images ever created, accessible anytime, anywhere, on a range of consumer devices. The public benefits of such universal libraries are overwhelming. They would provide unprecedented, online access to information, knowledge, and the fruits of human creativity for purposes of research, learning, and enjoyment. Further, seen in market terms, universal and fully accessible catalogues have become the product consumers demand.

Indeed, studies show that demand for universal and instant access is a primary motivator for individuals to engage in illicit file trading—as much or more of a motivator as avoiding payment for works that are legally available. As the Recording Industry Association of America has rightly recognized: "To be competitive, today's streaming, cloud and subscription music services require licenses to the full catalog of songs (and shares thereof) owned by virtually every music publisher."[19] That is increasingly true for other cultural goods as well. As one seasoned observer of the television industry presciently described the future of television: "Consumers don't care where or how they get their content. They don't care if it comes to them via cable, satellite, broadband, wi-fi, or wireless. They also don't care who provides the hardware (smart TV, set-top box, smartphone or tablet) to deliver the service that they want. They want an integrated, easy-to-use system to get their content. Period. This will include all the content currently available from the pay-TV operators, as well as Netflix, Amazon, Hulu, and even Yahoo."[20]

Short of some sort of compulsory blanket license, however, proprietary copyrights will leave huge gaps in online catalogs for music, movies, television shows, and other cultural works. We will be left with the current Netflix syndrome, in which major rights holders periodically pull their content to place it exclusively in their own proprietary distribution ventures. There are also millions of older works for which the copyright holder is unknown or it is unclear who holds the exclusive right to make the work available in digital format online. Without some form of compulsory license, those works cannot be made available by anybody without the risk of copyright infringement liability.

Second, markets for the production and distribution of information and creative expression tend to be highly concentrated. A handful of motion picture studios, television broadcasters, record labels, music publishers, book publishers, and scientific journal publishers control the vast majority of copyrighted works in their respective areas—and many of them are sister companies within multimedia conglomerate umbrellas. Markets for online aggregation and dissemination also tend to be highly concentrated: Witness Google, Apple, Facebook, and Amazon.

Even short of antitrust concerns, those high levels of market concentration call into question claims that voluntary copyright licensing meets consumer demand and serves the public interest. Concentrated markets tend to be rife with anticompetitive behavior and prices that are much higher than would be the case if markets were truly competitive. Proprietary copyrights exacerbate these tendencies. They give incumbents tools to suppress new media and new entrants to the market for distributing cultural works. And they give new online media giants opportunities for acquiring exclusive distribution rights from copyright holders.

By contrast, compulsory licensing would greatly diminish entry barriers for new media, to the benefit of consumers and, ultimately, creators of cultural expression. With compulsory licensing, any new media company could provide consumers digital access to movies, TV shows, music, or books so long as it paid the statutory rate. Studios, record labels, and publishers could not use exclusive rights to keep content behind their own paywall, seek to maintain their traditional dominance over content distribution, or favor new media giants.

The advantages to compulsory licensing do not overcome many authors' deeply felt objection that copyright law must recognize and protect their inherent right to control whether, by whom, and under what terms their creative product is distributed. Yet, compulsory licensing can provide practical benefits for authors as well as users. A properly configured compulsory licensing regime can guarantee authors a more certain source of revenue than can a proprietary copyright system. For example, Congress can structure statutory licenses so that a portion of the proceeds flows directly to creators and performers rather than being funneled through copyright industry intermediaries like record labels, which, creators and performers argue, unfairly divert the lion's share to themselves.

Moreover, statutory license regimes can be structured to preserve a degree of author control. For example, compulsory licenses might apply only to works for which the author has consented to initial public distribution. Authors could still prevent the distribution of unpublished works without their permission. In addition, Congress could amend the Copyright Act to give authors a moral right of authorship attribution. Such measures would at least partly compensate authors for the loss of proprietary control over further distribution.

Should consumers be able to watch television shows anytime and anywhere, while also automatically skipping commercials?

It is difficult to answer that question because the markets and media for viewing television and other video programming are so rapidly changing. Broadcasters currently look to three principal sources of revenue to fund television production: advertising, cable and satellite retransmission fees, and mobile television. Digital technology threatens to disrupt all three. And that disruption may assume monumental proportions should the current trend of consumers cutting the cord—terminating their cable and satellite subscriptions in favor of online video platforms—continue.

Advertising

In contrast to subscription cable and satellite television, over-the-air broadcast television is free in the sense that anyone with an antenna can watch it without having to purchase a subscription or make a payment to view any particular program. But in effect broadcast television audiences "pay" with their time and attention in watching commercials. Broadcaster advertising revenues depend on advertisers' assumption that television audiences will often watch commercials and, as a result, sometimes buy the advertised products.

Devices that make it easy for television viewers to skip commercials thus threaten broadcasters' advertising revenues. Granted, television viewers have long been able to avoid commercials by leaving the room or hitting the fast forwarding button on their TV remote. But those are fairly clumsy tools for viewers who wish to avoid commercials while not missing any of the TV program. As a result, in the predigital world, advertisers assumed that many, perhaps most, viewers would sit through commercials. Advertisers' rates thus reflected the estimated audience size for the television program.

By contrast, digital video recorders can be programmed to skip over commercials automatically. Dish Network's AutoHop feature is a prime example. AutoHop enables Dish subscribers to record primetime television shows and, with a single push of a button, automatically to skip over all commercials while watching a recorded show.

The broadcast networks—Fox, CBS, NBC, and ABC—each sued Dish over AutoHop. They asserted that Dish subscribers infringe broadcasters' copyright in television programming when subscribers record the programming and use AutoHop automatically to skip over commercials. The broadcasters further argued that Dish bears contributory liability for those infringements.

The courts ruled in favor of Dish. They reasoned that despite obvious differences between AutoHop and the Betamax, AutoHop users are still engaged in fair use time-shifting per the Supreme Court's 1984 ruling in *Sony v. Universal*. In particular, the U.S. Court of Appeals for the Ninth Circuit dismissed the broadcasters' argument that *Sony* should not apply when users automatically skip commercials and thus erode broadcasters' advertising revenue. The Ninth Circuit took the rather formalist position that skipping commercials does not implicate the broadcasters' copyright interest because the broadcaster does not own the copyright in the commercials that are skipped.

Dish's initial victories in court on copyright issues were short-lived. Like other satellite and cable operators, Dish cannot retransmit broadcasters' programming without the broadcasters' permission. (As I explain in the next section, broadcasters' right to prevent retransmission stems from federal telecommunications law.) ABC Disney successfully invoked its right to prevent Dish from retransmitting ABC Disney programming to pressure Dish to disable the AutoHop feature for the first three days after an ABC Disney TV show airs. In return, ABC Disney dismissed its copyright claims against Dish's AutoHop. Subsequently, as part of a settlement of Fox's copyright infringement lawsuit, Dish agreed to a seven-day delay for Fox programming. Consequently, Dish subscribers who are unwilling to wait the prescribed number of days to watch a TV show (including live sporting events) will not be able to skip commercials automatically. In turn, the broadcasters will be able to retain much of their advertising revenue.

Cable retransmission fees

For decades now, the vast majority of Americans have watched broadcast television as part of their paid cable or satellite television service, not by hooking up an antenna. That move to paid subscription television in lieu of the old rooftop or rabbit ears antenna raised the prospect of ruinous harm to broadcasters should subscription television services decline to carry some or all broadcast television programming. In 1992, Congress stepped in to ensure the continued viability of broadcast television. It enacted legislation requiring cable operators to carry local broadcast stations. That legislation was subsequently amended. As the law is currently formulated, broadcasters have the option in each local broadcast market of either: (1) requiring cable operators to carry their broadcasts in return for a statutory license fee in an amount determined under the Copyright Act; or (2) denying a cable operator the right to retransmit the broadcaster's broadcasts.

In most major television markets today, there is sufficient public demand for network and other broadcast television programming such that any cable operator that fails to carry broadcast programming would be at a significant competitive disadvantage. As a result, broadcasters are typically able to negotiate retransmission fees far in excess of the statutory license rates, backed by the threat of preventing the cable operator from retransmitting the broadcasters' programming at all. Disputes between broadcasters and cable operators over retransmission fees can leave cable subscribers without popular programming, such as when Fox threatened to pull its broadcasts—which included *American Idol* and National Football League games—from Time Warner Cable in 2009. Retransmission fees have thus come to be a significant supplement to advertising revenues for broadcasters.

More recently, broadcasters have achieved notable judicial success against a disruptive technology that threatened their cable retransmission revenues. Aereo, Inc. offered a service that enabled its subscribers to watch over-the-air television on any Internet-connected device. Aereo leased to each of its subscribers a remote mini-antenna and dedicated space on a computer server, both located at Aereo's facility. Subscribers could use the Aereo programming guide on their Internet-connected device to "watch" a program that was currently airing. In that event, the broadcast would be recorded as the subscriber watched, and the subscriber would view the program with a slight delay, but with the ability to pause or rewind the program as desired. Subscribers could also record broadcasts for later viewing, akin to a DVR.

For Aereo and its supporters, Aereo's service simply enabled its subscribers to do what they are legally entitled to do anyway: watch free over-the-air television and record it for later viewing. Of course, Aereo also made use of digital technology to offer significant advantages over previous technology. It freed its subscribers from reliance on television sets, rooftop or rabbit ears antenna, and cable and satellite carriers' expensive contracts. By contrast, the broadcasters countered that Aereo was performing the same function as cable television operators—retransmitting broadcast television to its subscribers—without paying the broadcast retransmission license fees required by the Copyright Act and federal telecommunications law. If Aereo were allowed to get away with doing that, the broadcasters further contended, cable television operators would also adopt Aereo's technology and business model, or at least insist on a substantial reduction in their retransmission fees.

The broadcasters' lawsuit against Aereo turned on a complex issue of statutory interpretation: whether Aereo was "publicly performing" copyrighted broadcast programming. It is clear that streaming programming online constitutes a "performance." The question in *Aereo* was whether Aereo was engaged in a "public" performance or merely making multiple private performances to individual subscribers. Only public performances fall within the copyright owner's exclusive rights.

Prior to the Aereo lawsuit, the U.S. Court of Appeals for the Second Circuit had ruled that cable operators do not "publicly perform" broadcast programming when their subscribers play programming that the subscribers have recorded on a remote DVR (essentially storage dedicated separately to each subscriber on the cable operator's computer server).

Following that precedent, Aereo argued that by transmitting programming via mini-antennas dedicated to each individual subscriber and via discrete recordings made for and by each individual subscriber, it was only facilitating multiple private performances, not publicly performing the programs. As a result, Aereo argued, it did not infringe the copyright owners' exclusive rights.

The Supreme Court ruled against Aereo on grounds that largely avoided the complex issues of statutory construction. The Court reasoned that no matter how Aereo had set up its system, Aereo functioned like a cable television operator that retransmits over-the-air television to its subscribers. And since Congress intended that any entity that functions like a cable television operator must pay retransmission fees to broadcasters and Aereo was not doing so, Aereo had infringed the broadcasters' copyrights.

Aereo and FilmOn X, a company offering a similar technology, then claimed that, based on the Supreme Court's reasoning, they should be classified as cable television operators and thus should fall within the statutory license for retransmissions of broadcast programming under the Copyright Act. The cable operators were steadfastly opposed. They did not want competition from companies that retransmit programming over the Internet. The broadcasters were also opposed because even if Aereo were to pay statutory license fees, they viewed Aereo and other new media that would like to stream programming over the Internet as a threat to broadcasters' much-anticipated third source of revenue: mobile TV.

The Copyright Office backed the cable operators and broadcasters. It maintained that Internet-based retransmission does not fall within the statutory license provisions for cable retransmission. The courts have now ruled conclusively against Aereo and FilmOn X. Most recently, the U.S. Court of Appeals for the Ninth Circuit held that the statutory language regarding cable retransmissions is ambiguous, but that it would defer to the Copyright Office's interpretation.[21]

Regardless of whether the Copyright Office's interpretation of the statutory license is correct, to discriminate against Internet retransmission cannot be justified as a matter of copyright policy. Copyright law should be neutral regarding which technological medium is used to produce, distribute, and enjoy creative expression. Copyright law certainly should not serve to stifle the new digital media to which consumers increasingly turn. Ideally, then, Congress should amend the retransmission statutory license provisions to include Internet retransmission, provided only that Internet retransmitters comply with pertinent Federal Communications Commission regulations that apply to cable systems.

Mobile TV

Consumers increasingly want to view television programming on their mobile devices—and broadcasters see mobile TV as a major source of future revenue. A number of companies—including major mobile carriers AT&T, Verizon, and Sprint—now offer mobile TV services through which consumers may watch streams of certain channels for a flat subscription rate and purchase other programming on a pay-per-view basis. The mobile carriers pay the broadcasters royalties for a negotiated license to provide such services. In addition, as of this writing, CBS and HBO have both announced live streaming services, through which subscribers may watch those channels on any Internet-connected device. Further, all the major broadcast networks offer per-program streaming services. (Of course, so do Netflix, Amazon, YouTube, and Vimeo, which are rapidly emerging as competitors to traditional broadcasters. More on them shortly.)

Mobile TV served as a prime motivation for broadcasters' successful efforts to quash Aereo and FilmOn X. Mobile TV also stood at the heart of a lawsuit that Fox brought against Dish Network. Fox contended that Dish's "Dish Anywhere" and "Hopper Transfers" technology infringes its copyrights. Those features enable Dish subscribers to watch on any

Internet-connected device both live television broadcasts and programs they have recorded on their DVR. Dish licenses the right to broadcast Fox programs to Dish subscribers' television sets via satellite. But in contrast to the mobile carriers' TV services, Dish does not pay Fox an additional license fee for transmitting Fox's programs to the Internet-connected device of the subscriber's choosing, wherever the Dish subscriber happens to be. Fox argued that the Dish features: (1) constitute a public performance under the Supreme Court's ruling in *Aereo*; and (2) enable consumer space-shifting, which Fox argued is not fair use, unlike the time-shifting countenanced in *Sony*. The courts largely ruled for Dish on those copyright issues, but for Fox on contract issues related to Dish's broadcast license agreement. The parties then settled the litigation.

Moving forward

The *Dish* and *Aereo* cases raise several issues of copyright law interpretation. Yet each presents a common underlying question: Should television broadcasters be able to use their copyrights to prevent disruptive technologies from undermining the broadcasters' current and anticipated revenue streams? From the consumer perspective, the disruptive technologies offer significant advantages. They enable consumers to view television broadcasts anytime, anywhere, on any Internet-connected device, and without watching commercials. But if the technologies are allowed to displace all three of broadcasters' principal revenue sources—advertising, retransmissions fees, and mobile TV licensing, what will remain of broadcast television?

The answer is that, even apart from copyright issues, digital technology will fundamentally disrupt broadcast television as we know it. The future of what we now call television will likely consist not of mobile TV, in the sense of television programming made available over digital networks, but, rather, of video content that is produced for a range of integrated and interconnected platforms, including computers, smartphones, tablets, and Internet-connected television sets. In that world, moreover, popular video content will come from a variety of sources, not just the major TV studios. Netflix's and Amazon's original programming are notable examples. Apple and Google have recently announced plans to enter the market for original programming as well.

In that scenario, established broadcast channels would largely fall by the wayside. Indeed, growing numbers of viewers, particularly young adults, are already jettisoning their cable and satellite subscriptions for online platforms that feature a broad menu of view-on-demand programming. These platforms include Netflix, Amazon, YouTube, and Vimeo—as well as infringing BitTorrent sites like Popcorn Time. Further, if copyright law and rights clearance licensing make it possible, we will see the emergence of online platforms that contain universal catalogues of video content and that enable consumers to interact with that content through social media. With digital technology, it is technologically feasible and economically efficient to establish searchable, interactive, and universal libraries of all television shows, movies, and other video content ever made. Like with recorded music today, consumers will come to demand sites that provide access to that universal—or near universal—video catalogue and that enable viewers to select which TV show or movie is streamed to their device whenever they want to watch it.

As video consumption moves to view-on-demand digital platforms, the issue of commercial skipping will also fade in importance. Advertisers are already deserting broadcast television for mobile platforms as viewers move to subscription-supported, advertising-free, any-device video viewing on services like Netflix.[22] That trend will only intensify in the future. Advertising revenue will come increasingly from advertising embedded in video programming and content-tailored social media. Advertisers will also look to banner ads, links, and the aggregation of data regarding individuals' viewing and buying preferences. In short, advertising markets for video platforms will be more akin to the Google and Facebook models than current broadcast television commercials—and digital media companies like Google and Facebook are more adept at extracting full value from those markets than are today's movie studios and television broadcasters.

Copyright law should not stand in the way of the transition to new viewing habits and platforms. It should aim to ensure, through a combination of exclusive rights and statutory licenses, both that video producers have robust economic incentives to create new expression and that new technology platforms for video viewing are not stifled by incumbent copyright industries. Today's music streaming sites, featuring large catalogues of recorded music from a broad variety of sources, are made possible by a complex combination of compulsory and voluntary content licenses—as well as competition from pirate sites that push content owners to come to terms with licensed streaming platforms. That regime is far from perfect. Nonetheless, it might serve as a rough model for television, movies, and other video content in the future. In any event, copyright law should be designed to foster diverse creative expression and widespread dissemination of content through a variety of media, not to entrench any particular business model or industry.

Should copyright law permit mass digitization to establish publicly available digital archives?

A number of projects are underway to digitize books on a mass scale with the hope of creating a universal digital library of all books ever written. Archives have also initiated projects to digitize large quantities of legacy images, sound recordings, pamphlets, and motion pictures. A universal digital library would bring immense public benefits. It would make the wealth of human knowledge, opinion, and creative imagination far more accessible to libraries, schools, researchers, and readers the world over, particularly those who lack ready access to major university research libraries. Digital archives also make possible valuable new scholarly research. For example, scholars can employ digital search to scour a database of digitized books to determine when certain terms and phrases came into popular use. Finally, mass digitization could provide authors and publishers of older, out-of-print works with new audiences, markets, and sources of income.

None of the mass digitization projects has received as much attention—or aroused as much controversy—as the Google Books Library project. Google contracted with some twenty major university and public libraries to scan millions of books in those libraries' collections. Google has created a searchable database of the books' entire texts, accessible through Google's advertising-supported search engine. Google makes the entire text of public domain books available for viewing or download. It also displays portions of many in-copyright books under terms of licenses with major publishers. Finally, in response to user search queries, Google displays short snippets (amounting to about three sentences each) of in-copyright books that have not been licensed for greater viewing by the publisher. Google also displays bibliographical information and locations where users might obtain a copy of the book.

Major publishers and the Authors Guild sued Google and its library partners for scanning entire books for inclusion in the searchable database. The Authors Guild's lawsuit was certified as a class action representing all authors holding U.S. copyright interests in one or more books. The publishers settled their claim, but the Authors Guild went to court—and lost. The U.S. Court of Appeals for the Second Circuit held that scanning entire books to include them in a searchable database is fair use, at least so long as only short snippets are displayed to users.

The Second Circuit ruling enables Google (and others) to create a digital database of scanned books in order to provide something like a value-added, online card catalogue—an information location tool that informs readers about what books might be relevant to their interests. However, that search tool falls far short of a universal digital library, where millions of books—representing the entire corpus of published knowledge—would be instantly available, in their entirety, to anyone with an Internet connection.

The proposed terms of a class action settlement in the Google Books litigation would have made a momentous step in the direction of a universal digital library. As fashioned by Google, leading book publishers, and the Authors Guild, the settlement would have permitted Google to make available the entire text of all out-of-print books, with various arrangements for royalties and with provisions for rights holders to opt out. Google could have charged for online access. But all of the books would have also been available for free at terminals to be placed in every local library that wanted one. In addition, Google would have continued to make available portions of in-print books with the copyright owner's permission and the full text of public domain books, as it does today.

However, class action settlements cannot take effect without judicial approval—and the presiding court refused to accept such a far-reaching settlement, one that would have countenanced an exponentially greater degree of display and distribution by Google than the online card catalogue for which Google was sued in the first place. In so ruling, the court reasoned that such a settlement would, in effect, implement a major reworking of copyright law in the area of mass digitization. Such a significant change, the court held, should be the exclusive province of Congress, not private parties in a court-approved settlement. The court also rejected the settlement proposal because it would have given one party—Google— a significant advantage over competitors. Since Google's competitors were not parties to the settlement, they would still face the risk of copyright infringement liability if they were to embark on a similar project. Finally, the court noted that the proposed settlement would have reversed the default "opt-in" rule under copyright law. Under the opt-in rule, one who wishes to reproduce and publicly distribute a copyrighted work must obtain the copyright holder's permission in advance of doing so, regardless of whether a book is out of print or the copyright owner is known. But the proposed settlement would have allowed Google to scan books without advance permission. A book's rights holder could always require Google to remove the book from Google's searchable database. But Google would not be liable for copyright infringement so long as it promptly removed the book upon the rights holder's request.

Following the demise of the Google Books class action settlement, it is now up to Congress to consider a copyright reform that enables any entity, not just Google, to engage in the mass digitization of predigital works to create a publicly available digital archive. To that end, the Copyright Office issued a discussion document on mass digitization.[23] The Office set out three possible legal frameworks for Congress to consider: (1) voluntary licensing, pursuant to which digital archives would have to obtain advance copyright holder consent to digitize any copyrighted work; (2) extended collective licensing, pursuant to which the law would establish a collective licensing organization representing all authors of a given type of work to negotiate with digital archives, subject to regulatory oversight and authors' right to withdraw from the licensing organization; and (3) statutory licensing.

Whatever the relative merits of those three legal frameworks, the Copyright Office discussion document ignores an important fact: the legal barriers to mass digitization of legacy books, movies, and sound recordings are largely of Congress' own ill-considered making. Were prior U.S. copyright law still in force, the bulk of out-of-print works would now be in the public domain. Under the Copyright Act of 1909, copyrights in published works lasted only twenty-eight years unless renewed for a second copyright term—and the vast majority of copyrights were not renewed. But today, following enactment of the Copyright Act of 1976 and subsequent amendments, copyrights typically last for ninety-five years or more, with no renewal requirement. As a result, many millions of out-of-print works remain protected by copyright.

At the very least, Congress should remove the barrier to mass digitization that it has created. Short of reinstituting a full-fledged copyright renewal requirement, Congress could do that by establishing an opt-out regime for mass digitization and digital archives loosely modeled on the previous two-term copyright system.

The bare bones outline of such a regime would be as follows: the Copyright Act would be amended to provide a copyright exception that generally permits the digitization and inclusion in an online digital archive of any work first made public more than twenty-eight years ago. However, copyright owners would have the right to override that exception by registering an appropriate opt-out notice with the Copyright Office. Legacy works subject to an opt-out notice could be included in a publicly available digital archive only with the copyright holder's advance consent. Copyright owners who initially fail to register such an opt-out notice could still opt out at a later time, but they would also have to notify any digital archive from which they wish their legacy works removed. Upon receiving such a notice, the digital archive would be required to remove the work. But it would not have to pay the copyright owner compensation for the prior use. Further, even if the copyright owner opts out, archivists' value-added online card catalogues, including those that display snippets in response to search queries, would continue to be privileged fair use, following the judicial ruling in the Google Books litigation.

Such an opt-out regime for mass digitization would fall short of laying the groundwork for universal libraries. But it would enable digital archives to feature millions of legacy in-copyright works in their entirety, in addition to public domain works and works that are included under the terms of a copyright owner license. At the same time, such an opt-out regime would give copyright owners the right to withhold their works from any mass digitization project, or to negotiate a license for including a work in the digital archive. As such, the regime would obtain many of the benefits of mass digitization while preserving copyright holders' ability to assert their exclusive rights.

Ideally, however, Congress should go further than merely removing the barriers to mass digitization that are of its own making. Congress should also affirmatively promote the creation of universal digital libraries. Congress could do so by providing for statutory licensing for including legacy works in digital archives that make such works available only for personal, noncommercial perusal. The license might be limited to works first made public more than twenty-eight years ago to avoid interfering with markets for newly created works. Further, the statutory license could be narrowly tailored to allow only online viewing or listening—or having access to a digital copy for a limited period of time, akin to borrowing a hardcopy book from a library.

Under that proposal, copyright owners could not prevent digital archives from making digital copies of their works in order to make them available for the limited uses permitted under the statutory license. Copyright owners' rights would be limited to receiving compensation for digital archives' inclusion of their works in amounts determined pursuant to the terms of the statutory license.

VI

COPYRIGHT IN THE
INTERNATIONAL ARENA

Copyright markets are global in scope. U.S.-based copyright industries (some of which are multinational conglomerates) earn a significant share of their revenues from exports. Social media also transcend national borders. So do notorious file-sharing sites like Pirate Bay.

United States copyright industries complain bitterly that piracy in foreign countries such as China rob them of potential revenues. They also point to foreign websites as a significant source of infringing content that flows into the United States. Not surprisingly, therefore, the debates about copyright reach these cross-border markets, uses, and infringement.

How does copyright law apply in the global marketplace?

There is no international copyright law per se. Rather each country has its own copyright law, with its own unique jurisprudence and rules. Each country's laws govern questions of copyright infringement within that country's borders.

To illustrate, consider this hypothetical example. Say that Universal Studios produces a movie in the United States called *Godzilla Goes to Law School*. And say that Universal wishes to prevent a Brazilian movie studio from producing and distributing in Brazil an unlicensed sequel to that movie, called

Godzilla Becomes a Lawyer. To do so, Universal would have to sue the Brazilian movie studio for infringement of Universal's Brazilian copyrights under Brazilian copyright law. Moreover, unless a U.S. court has jurisdiction over the Brazilian studio and is willing to exercise its jurisdiction to consider a claim for infringement under Brazilian copyright law, Universal will have to bring its lawsuit in Brazil. (The jurisdictional issues depend on various factors, which are too complex to discuss here.)

In any event, it would be Brazilian law, not U.S. copyright law, that determines whether Universal owns a Brazilian copyright in *Godzilla Goes to Law School*. On that score, a Brazilian court might refuse to recognize the work-for-hire doctrine under which Universal claims to own the copyright under U.S. copyright law. Brazilian law would also govern whether making a sequel of a movie infringes the copyright in the original movie. The answer is by no means obvious. Making a sequel often involves using some of the same characters that appear in the original movie, but none of the original movie's dialogue, settings, or storyline. Brazilian copyright law might come to different doctrinal results than U.S. copyright law on such questions. Further, perhaps Brazilian copyright law only protects works created by Brazilian nationals or accords lesser protection for works created by U.S. nationals than by Brazilian nationals. (That's just a hypothetical; in fact Brazil does not discriminate against U.S. works in its copyright law, but some other countries, like Iran, do.)

That is not the end of the story. Although each country has its own distinct copyright law, there are a number of multilateral and bilateral treaties that govern international copyright relations. These treaties typically forbid countries that are party to the treaty to discriminate against foreign nationals in their copyright laws. They also require that treaty partners provide specified minimum rights for foreign authors even if the country's own nationals enjoy lesser rights.

A prime example is the Berne Convention for the Protection of Literary and Artistic Works, a treaty initially adopted in 1886 and to which more than 160 countries are now parties. The Berne Convention requires, among other things, that each Berne Convention country provide nationals from other Berne Convention countries at least the same rights under copyright law that that country provides its own nationals. In addition, the Berne Convention requires that each country must provide foreign authors certain "minimum rights," including the exclusive right to authorize reproductions, adaptations, and public performances of their works even if it does not provide its own authors with those rights. The Berne Convention also requires that the copyright term for foreign authors be a minimum of the life of the author plus fifty years (with some exceptions). Importantly, the Berne Convention and other such treaties do not require countries to grant minimum rights to their own authors. Rather the treaties obligate countries only with respect to expressive works and nationals from other countries that are party to the treaty.

Moreover, countries' obligations under the treaties flow to each other, not to private parties. Hence, a private party like Universal Studios would not have any direct recourse if a country violates its obligations under a copyright treaty. Rather, if Brazil's copyright law should fall short of Brazil's Berne Convention obligations, Universal would have to petition the U.S. government to attempt to induce Brazil to comply with the treaty, whether by diplomacy or bringing a complaint against Brazil in the appropriate international tribunal.

How do other countries' copyright laws differ from U.S. copyright law?

U.S. copyright law has traditionally differed significantly from the copyright law of most other countries. U.S. copyright law flows from the idea that copyrights are necessary to give authors a financial incentive to produce creative expression that benefits society as a whole. In that view, copyright is a limited monopoly that Congress grants to authors to serve a public benefit, not merely to reward authors for their own sake. In line with that traditional understanding, U.S. copyright law long provided that copyright protection comes into effect only if: (1) the author makes his or her work available to the public; and (2) affirmatively claims the copyright by affixing a copyright notice on all published copies. Further, U.S. authors have long had to apply to the Copyright Office to obtain a copyright registration in order to enforce their copyright in court. In addition, U.S. copyrights lasted for a short time compared to today's copyright term. Prior to the Copyright Act of 1976, copyrights lasted for just twenty-eight years from publication unless the copyright owner renewed the copyright for another twenty-eight-year term. Congress enacted a copyright term of the life of the author plus fifty years as part of the Copyright Act of 1976 to make the U.S. copyright term consistent with the copyright term requirement of the Berne Convention.

By contrast, European countries recognize copyright as an inherent, natural right of the author, akin to a property right in chattel or land. Under that "authors' rights" approach, copyrights last for the author's life plus some term of years and arise automatically upon the work's creation, without any need to comply with formalities like registration or notice. Authors also have moral rights by which they may exercise and enforce their personal right to control the manner and form in which their work is presented to the public even if they have transferred their economic interest in the work to a publisher, label, or studio. Many countries have adopted the European authors' rights approach. These include many former colonies of European countries and countries, like Japan, that fashioned their own copyright law on the European model.

The United Kingdom and countries such as Australia and Canada that more or less follow the U.K. copyright tradition lie somewhere between the United States and Continental European approaches. But through their Berne

Convention obligations, they have adopted certain aspects of the Continental European approach, including moral rights. Indeed, as noted above, the Berne Convention—to which the United States acceded in 1989—also bears some influence on U.S. copyright law.

Finally, many developing countries have traditionally had minimal copyright protection and enforcement. This partly stems from an ideology that authors' creations are the common heritage of humankind, not the property of an individual. Developing countries' minimal copyright protection also originates in a perceived national interest in gaining cheap access to foreign informational and cultural works. Developing and emerging countries' minimal copyright protection and enforcement has been a source of great frustration for copyright industries in the United States, Europe, and elsewhere in the developed world.

Why do some countries tolerate copyright "pirates"?

When the United States was a young, developing country, our copyright law did not provide any copyright protection for foreign works. Indeed, Congress did not extend copyright protection to foreign works until 1891. The reason for the lack of protection for foreign works through most of the nineteenth century was that Congress perceived it to be in the national interest for Americans to have cheap access to foreign knowledge and literature. In addition, American publishers did a brisk business issuing reprints of British books, free of any legal obligation to obtain permission or pay copyright royalties to the author.

Not surprisingly, many of today's developing and emerging countries see copyright in the same way. In their view, to grant copyright protection for foreign works would be contrary to their national interest in gaining unhindered, cheap access to foreign knowledge and cultural expression. In addition, local "pirate" industries are significant sources of revenue, employment, and tax payments in some developing countries.

One would expect third world countries to favor stronger copyright protection when their indigenous creative industries develop, particularly when they begin to export their creative works to other countries. In the United States in the late nineteenth century, American authors lobbied heavily to accord copyright protection to foreign works so publishers would cease favoring works of foreign authors to whom they did not have to pay royalties. And as the United States became an exporter of creative works, political pressure increased to provide strong copyright protection to foreign works in the United States so that other countries would similarly protect American authors and copyright industries. But absent a robust domestic copyright industry, developing countries are unlikely to enthusiastically accord copyright protection for foreign works.

What treaties govern copyright in the international arena?

Beginning in the mid-nineteenth century, two factors combined to spur diplomatic efforts to adopt bilateral and multilateral copyright treaties: differences in countries' copyright laws and countries' propensity to provide little or no protection to works of foreigners. Then as now, early copyright treaties typically prohibited discrimination against foreign authors and required certain minimum rights for foreign authors.

The premiere multilateral copyright treaty is the Berne Convention for the Protection of Literary and Artistic Works, discussed in the previous questions. Although the Berne Convention was adopted in 1886, the United States did not become a party until 1989, over a century later. The primary reason for that long delay was the presence of authors' rights-inspired provisions in the Berne Convention that were seen to stand in blatant contradiction to U.S. copyright tradition. These included Berne provisions prohibiting the imposition of formalities like a copyright notice and registration as a condition to copyright protection, requiring protection for the moral rights of attribution and integrity, and requiring that copyrights last for at least the life of the author plus fifty years. The United States' much-belated decision to adhere to the Berne Convention arose largely out of pragmatic concerns: the United States could hardly insist that other countries accord greater copyright protection to U.S. works if the United States was not a party to the world's premiere multilateral copyright treaty. Indeed, by the time it acceded to the Berne Convention in 1989, the United States was engaged in intensive multilateral trade negotiations that led to the establishment of the World Trade Organization (WTO) and, at the initiative of the United States and other developed countries, the inclusion of intellectual property within that world trade regime. The Agreement on Trade-Related Aspects of Intellectual Property Rights (TRIPS) is an integral part of the agreement establishing the WTO. Hence, any country that becomes a member of the WTO must adhere to TRIPS.

TRIPS incorporates by reference the substantive provisions of the Berne Convention, except—at the United States' insistence—Berne's provisions requiring protection for authors' moral rights. TRIPS also imposes additional "Berne-plus" obligations for protecting and enforcing copyrights that are more stringent than those of the Berne Convention. Further, TRIPS subjects WTO members to a dispute settlement procedure that can result in the levying of trade sanctions against a country that violates its TRIPS obligations. (However, TRIPS also contains a moratorium for least-developed countries to give them time to bring their copyright laws and enforcement up to TRIPS standards. The moratorium has been repeatedly extended and remains in effect.)

Soon after TRIPS was adopted in 1994, the United States again took the initiative to strengthen copyright enforcement worldwide. This time the United States pushed for adoption of a new treaty designed to bring the Berne Convention into the digital age.[1] The United States and European Union supported a draft of that treaty that would further ratchet up countries' obligations to protect copyright and that would sharply curtail permissible exceptions to copyright holder rights. The initiative transpired within the framework of the World Intellectual Property Organization (WIPO), a special agency of the United Nations that administers the Berne Convention.

The U.S. efforts culminated in the adoption of two treaties in December 1996: the WIPO Copyright Treaty and the WIPO Performances and Phonograms Treaty. The WIPO Copyright Treaty makes clear that rights holders must be given the exclusive right to stream their works from websites. It also requires that treaty parties "provide adequate legal protection and effective legal remedies against the circumvention of" technological protection measures designed to enforce rights guaranteed by the WIPO Copyright Treaty or Berne Convention. On the other hand, the Treaty also reflects developing countries' pushback against efforts to ratchet up copyright protection. It recognizes, for the first time in a multilateral copyright treaty, "the need to maintain a balance between the rights of authors and the larger public interest." The Treaty also recognizes that countries may devise new exceptions and limitations to copyrights that are appropriate in the digital network environment.

Finally, the United States has entered into more than a dozen bilateral and regional free trade agreements—and is negotiating another dozen or so such agreements—that include provisions requiring copyright protection. The United States has used these agreements as a vehicle to impose obligations that would further increase the duration and scope of copyrights, beyond what is required under the Berne Convention or TRIPS. The bilateral and regional trade agreements also lock in recent copyright expansions in U.S. law—even when those expansions remain subject to considerable dispute in the United States. For example, bilateral and regional agreements typically require the parties to provide for a copyright term of the life of the author plus seventy years and to provide for protections against circumvention of technological protection measures akin to those set out in the DMCA (even though the DMCA provides greater rights to copyright holders than required by the WIPO treaties). These free trade agreements have become increasingly controversial, especially since they are typically negotiated without revealing the draft provisions to the public prior to presentation to Congress for an up or down vote.

How are the battles over copyright impacted by events and laws outside the United States?

We live in an age of global markets and communications networks. Hence, it is not surprising that debates over U.S. copyright policy extend to how our copyright law should address piracy emanating from abroad and how our government should seek greater copyright protection for American movies, television shows, sound recordings, software, print publications, and other such products in other countries.

The international dimension enters the debates over copyright in a number of ways. For example, among the controversial provisions of the now-defunct Stop Online Piracy Act were those that could have required U.S. Internet intermediaries to block access to foreign websites that house infringing content. In addition, the copyright industries regularly trumpet their contribution to the U.S. balance of trade as reason for strengthening copyright protection in this country and putting pressure on other countries to do the same.

The copyright industries also highlight what they claim is the devastating effect on their profitability of massive piracy in some foreign countries. Massive piracy abroad no doubt deprives copyright industries of revenues that they might otherwise have earned. Further, foreign websites featuring pirated content are a prime source of such content in the United States.

Unfortunately, however, copyright industries have regularly presented estimates of monetary harm due to piracy that defy credibility. For example, it is obvious that only a small fraction of pirated copies displace the market for legitimate copies in developing and emerging countries. Consumers in those countries could never afford to pay the copyright industry price for all pirated copies that are currently given away for free or sold at a low price. Nonetheless, copyright industry lobbyists' estimates of monetary harm have too often assumed that every pirated copy supplants what would otherwise be a lawful sale. No less unfortunately, government reports frequently repeat questionable copyright industry numbers.

In that regard, the copyright industries have exerted considerable influence on U.S. policy toward global copyright enforcement. Acting primarily through the Department of Commerce and the Office of the United States Trade Representative (USTR), the United States aggressively encourages the adoption and implementation of high levels of copyright protection and enforcement around the world. The USTR, for example, prepares an annual report on the adequacy and effectiveness of other countries' intellectual property rights protection and enforcement. The USTR report features watch lists of countries that the USTR deems to be inadequate protectors of intellectual property, with the threat that the United States might levy trade sanctions against those who do not implement high levels of protection.

In its reports, the USTR regularly takes countries to task for what it views as overly liberal uses of statutory licensing, inadequate protection against circumventing technological protection measures, and failure to institute a procedure that requires Internet service providers to accede to copyright owner takedown notices. As we have seen, such matters are subject to considerable debate within the United States when it comes to domestic U.S. copyright law and policy. Nonetheless, the USTR typically parrots the position of copyright industry trade associations in assessing other countries' copyright laws. The USTR also publishes an annual "Notorious Markets List," designed to focus the "fight against global piracy and counterfeiting of American products." The Notorious Markets

List includes markets that facilitate online infringement via "pay-per-download" services, BitTorrent indexing, and BitTorrent tracking.

In addition to the USTR reports, over the last three decades, the United States has been active in negotiating and entering into a network of multilateral, regional, and bilateral treaties and trade agreements that are either focused on copyright or that include copyright provisions as part of a broader trade agreement. Those treaties and agreements impose obligations on foreign countries to provide greater copyright protection and enforcement for U.S. works. But since they impose reciprocal obligations on the United States, the treaties and trade agreements serve as a double-edged sword. Copyright industry supporters use them strategically to insist upon expanded rights under U.S. copyright law. Indeed, copyright industry trade associations have repeatedly sought to obtain treaty provisions that are *more* favorable to them than legislative enactments that they have been able to obtain in the United States. Once those provisions are part of a treaty signed by the United States, the copyright industries turn around and lobby Congress to amend the Copyright Act, purportedly as needed to comply with the treaty.

For example, the DMCA anti-circumvention provisions, which Congress enacted in 1998, were framed as amendments needed to implement anticipated U.S. obligations under the WIPO Copyright Treaty of 1996 (which the Senate eventually ratified in 1999). In fact, however, the DMCA anti-circumvention provisions granted copyright holders far greater rights than required under the Treaty. For example, the DMCA prohibits circumvention of technological protection measures used to control *access* to copyrighted works. It does not just prohibit circumvention of technological protection measures used to prevent copying and other copyright infringements, as is required by the Treaty.

Likewise, copyright industry associations and others have repeatedly invoked supposed U.S. treaty obligations to oppose exceptions and limitations to copyrights in the United

States. They assert, for example, that statutory licensing and a robust fair use privilege run afoul of U.S. treaty obligations that limit permissible exceptions and limitations to copyright. Space does not permit further discussion here, but suffice it to say that—like characterizing the DMCA anti-circumvention provisions as necessary to "implement" the WIPO Copyright Treaty—such claims are often greatly overstated and not to be taken at face value.

VII

"THE NEXT GREAT COPYRIGHT ACT"

HOW MIGHT COPYRIGHT BE REFORMED?

What is copyright reform?

The term "copyright reform" connotes a significant modification or full-scale revision of the Copyright Act. Congress typically entertains the possibility of copyright reform when new technologies for disseminating creative expression have rendered the existing Copyright Act inadequate or obsolete.

Our current copyright statute, the Copyright Act of 1976, was such a revision. It replaced and substantially modified the Copyright Act of 1909. Congress enacted the 1909 Act at the dawn of the sound recording and motion picture industries but before the advent of commercial radio and television broadcasting, cable and satellite television, and computer programs. As a result, courts struggled to apply antiquated provisions of the 1909 Act to those later technologies and the new markets for creative expression they made possible.

Yet the Copyright Act of 1976 did not just address new technologies. It also effected a major conceptual shift in U.S. copyright law. The 1976 Act adopted a more author-centric approach and moved U.S. copyright law in the direction of compliance with the Berne Convention for the Protection of Literary and Artistic Works. As such, the 1976 Act accorded federal copyright protection to unpublished as well as published works. It also made the copyright term a single unitary term of the life of the author plus fifty years rather than a binary term that required the copyright owner to register a copyright renewal at the end of twenty-eight years. Finally, the 1976 Act codified the fair use privilege and sharply limited the circumstances in which the work-for-hire doctrine applies to commissioned works.

As Jessica Litman has detailed, much of the Copyright Act of 1976 reflects compromises hammered out in exhaustive negotiations among interested stakeholders, including copyright industries, broadcasters and cablecasters, authors' associations, and libraries.[1] Indeed, key members of Congress repeatedly pushed the affected players to hammer out draft statutory language reflecting their compromise consensus.

To this day, Congress continues to lean on the affected industries to negotiate and draft copyright reform provisions. For example, the Digital Millennium Copyright Act of 1998 (DMCA) implemented a grand bargain between the copyright and telecommunications industries with regard to copyright and digital media. It prohibited the circumvention of technological protection measures that control access to copyrighted works. At the same time, it gave Internet intermediaries a broad safe harbor against liability for users' infringements. In so doing, the DMCA put into place the notice and takedown system under which Internet service providers respond to copyright holder notices of infringement by taking down thousands of infringing copies every day.

Are we due for another copyright reform?

Many observers believe so. They reason that the Copyright Act of 1976, as amended from time to time, has failed to keep pace with the explosive growth of global digital networks, user-generated content, mobile data communications, peer-to-peer file sharing, and platforms for mass digitization and aggregation of near-universal catalogues of music, video, and text.

The Copyright Act of 1976 was intended to be forward looking and, to the extent possible, technologically neutral. For example, the Act defines "copies" as "material objects . . . in which a work is fixed by any method now known or later developed." Further, the DMCA was meant to assure copyright industries that they could make their works available online without facing massive infringement, while assuring telecommunications firms that they could provide Internet services free from the risk of copyright liability for their users' infringements. Likewise, in the 1990s Congress enacted and refined a digital performance right in sound recordings to ensure that record labels would have a viable market for sound recordings in the digital age, while making the labels' new right subject to a statutory license to make way for the then-nascent industries of webcasting and satellite radio.

Nevertheless, the onslaught of new technologies and platforms for disseminating creative expression leads many to believe that piecemeal amendments are inadequate. Most notably, in her prior position as Register of Copyrights, Maria A. Pallante called for a new comprehensive review and revision of U.S. copyright law, leading to the enactment of what she colorfully termed "the next great Copyright Act."[2] The Copyright Principles Project, headed by UC Berkeley professor Pamela Samuelson, has also set out a number of guidelines and specific proposals for copyright law reform.[3] More recently, the House Judiciary Committee held a series of hearings to engage in a comprehensive review of the Copyright Act and to consider proposals for reform.

Not surprisingly, proposals for reform differ radically in specifics, depending on who is making the proposal. For some, copyright reform is all about bolstering copyright enforcement, both civil and criminal. In that view, the Copyright Act must provide far more effective means to make certain that "people with malicious intent" cannot "profit from the creativity of others without providing appropriate compensation," as determined by the marketplace, not the government.[4] At the other end of the spectrum, some call for replacing copyright's exclusive rights with a system of statutory licensing, private copying levies, and government subsidies for artistic expression.

To its great credit, the Copyright Principles Project brought together scholars and stakeholders with diverse perspectives and aimed to overcome the heated rhetoric that regularly colors copyright debates. But while the Project participants reached consensus on the principles that must underlie copyright law and on a number of specific reform proposals, there remained fundamental questions, such as how to define copyright's exclusive rights, on which they could not agree. For example, Project participants shared the view that truly noncommercial, personal uses that cause no market harm to the copyright owner should be exempt from infringement liability. But they differed on which uses should fall within that category, how the burden of proof on market harm should be allocated, and how, if at all, copyright's exclusive rights should be redefined to implement that principle.

In sum, whatever the need for copyright reform, achieving the level of agreement required to enact it faces significant challenges. I return to that issue at the end of this chapter.

When should copyright policy be based on empirical evidence?

Whenever possible! Copyright reform must rest on solid empirical evidence about how copyright law impacts authors, users, and the copyright market.

Unfortunately, the copyright debate is too often grounded in heated rhetoric, flimsy data, and speculative conclusions that have little basis in solid empirical evidence. The same is true of copyright policymaking and lawmaking. Reports of congressional committees and other government agencies regularly lend credence to highly skewed data produced by industry lobbyists. Thanks to digital technology, much of the data needed to develop empirical evidence on copyright is generated in the course of online uses of copyrighted works, digital tracking and copyright licensing, and allocation of licensing proceeds to authors. But that data largely resides in the private sector. It is held by copyright industries, collective rights management organizations, Internet service providers, search engines, and social media. Too often, industry spokespersons and lobbyists release proprietary data selectively, to support their side of the battles over copyright.

In the vacuum left by the paucity of reliable data, participants in hearings before the Copyright Office, Department of Commerce, Department of Justice, and congressional committees repeatedly espouse what can only be described as "faith-based" arguments for according copyright holders broader and longer exclusive rights. Authors, they declare, have the inherent right to control their "property." Exceptions to copyright constitute "trespass." Voluntary licensing and "free market" bargaining are the obvious solution to copyright's ills. No matter that copyright licensing markets are notoriously subject to market failure. Or that copyright markets tend to be highly concentrated and have been the subject of antitrust authorities' repeated investigation of industry collusion. On the other side of the copyright debate, blithe and unsubstantiated assertions about the ability of copyright industries to prosper in a universe of massive file sharing "just like the motion picture industry adapted to the videocassette recorder" are equally lacking in empirical support.

Copyright's primary purpose is to serve the public benefit by providing an economic incentive for the creation and dissemination of creative expression from a diversity of sources. Accordingly, Congress must tailor copyright law to spur creation of new works while providing widespread public access to works that have already been created. Lawmakers face a daunting task in determining the right balance in the face of rapidly changing technologies for the creation and distribution of cultural expression and the fundamental disruption of copyright industries that such change has wrought. At the very least, lawmakers should be guided by solid empirical data concerning questions that underlie proposals for copyright reform.

Many such questions cry out for greater empirical analysis. For example, how do digital technologies impact the creation, dissemination, and use of different types of creative expression? Which types of works would be created and disseminated even without copyright's economic incentive and which would be undersupplied? What are the costs of increasing copyright enforcement? What are the relative costs of imposing filtering and policing obligations on Internet service providers versus the costs of repeat infringements under our current DMCA safe harbor? Does the availability of illicit file-sharing networks depress copyright owners' revenue from licensed streaming services and social media? What are the relative contributions to the national economy of cultural industries and new technological media? How does the need to clear a multiplicity of copyrights impede copyright licensing? To what extent could non-copyright sources of revenue, including targeted online advertising, make up for diminished copyright enforcement? Are authors best served by current copyright industries or does digital technology provide plausible vehicles for authors to make a living by disseminating directly to audiences or through new intermediaries?

Copyright reform requires answers to these questions and many more critical empirical questions along similar lines. Even if—as some observers argue—authors have an inherent right to control their creative expression, it is incumbent on lawmakers to confront the social costs and benefits of giving legal recognition to that right. After all, fundamental rights are rarely absolute. Every democratic legal system balances fundamental rights, such as the right to free speech, privacy, and reputation, against other rights and the public interest.

What are the advantages and disadvantages of alternative compensation systems?

"Alternative compensation systems" are mechanisms for compensating creators and copyright holders for uses of copyrighted works without requiring copyright holder permission for the use. Copyright laws generally give copyright holders the right to withhold permission for others' uses. They thus require users to negotiate licenses to make use of copyright works. By contrast, alternative compensation systems provide creators and copyright holders only with compensation, not the right to forbid use.

Alternative compensation systems have long been a feature of the U.S. copyright system. They include statutory licenses for cover recordings, broadcast retransmissions, and webcasting. The levy imposed on digital music recording equipment and media as well as the compulsory license for music performances under the ASCAP and BMI antitrust decrees are additional examples. Alternative compensation systems are also a central feature of copyright law in other countries. For example, some countries provide for private copying levies. These permit individual copying of purchased content but impose levies on copying equipment and media. Others impose a variety of compulsory licenses.

In addition, alternative compensation systems often involve mandatory or "extended" collective licensing. In that instance, the law provides that a single collective management organization bargains and grants copyright licenses on behalf of all rights holders in the relevant sector. No such mandatory collective management organizations operate in the United States; membership in organizations like ASCAP and SoundExchange is voluntary. But a number of European countries provide for a single organization to represent all rights holders in a given area, such as public performances of music, and regulate that organization's operations accordingly. A single mandatory collective management organization could clearly garner anticompetitive market power in bargaining for licensing fees with prospective users. As a result, like ASCAP and BMI, the organization's licensing rates and practices are typically regulated by the government, and the organization must grant licenses at approved rates. In those instances, mandatory collective licensing effectively becomes yet another alternative compensation system.

Proposals for additional alternative compensation systems abound. They include proposals in which a levy would be imposed on Internet access, with the levy proceeds distributed to rights holders. Other proposals include voluntary user payments and funding creators through government grants and rewards.

All such alternative compensation systems substitute for proprietary copyrights to one degree or another. Usually, an administrative or judicial body determines the amount that users must pay, in accordance with a formula proscribed in the copyright statute. In some systems, however, creators receive compensation from general tax funds or voluntary contributions. Either way, proceeds are typically allocated to rights holders, through collective rights management organizations, according to the extent to which works are used. By contrast, some alternative compensations provide funding for creators without regard to relative user demand for each work.

Consider, for example, proposals for a file-trading levy. A file-trading levy would allow noncommercial peer-to-peer file trading. And since users would be allowed to trade files, providers of file-trading platforms and other Internet intermediaries would face no liability for users' file trading. In return, however, copyright law would impose a levy on Internet access and, possibly, other services and equipment that consumers use to engage in file trading. The levy proceeds would then be allocated among creators and copyright holders in accordance with statistical sampling of which works are being traded. A copyright office tribunal or some other administrative body could determine the amount of the levy to be imposed. To do that, the tribunal would use a statutory standard, such as the fair income/fair return standard, that takes into account the relative contributions of creators, copyright-holding intermediaries, and providers of products and services that are subject to the levy.

Greater deployment of alternative compensation systems would offer significant advantages over the current copyright regime. Those systems enable new media efficiently to disseminate large volumes of works for which the negotiated license fee for each individual work would be quite small. They also prevent copyright industries or any single copyright holder from engaging in strategic holdout—refusing to grant a license unless the new media pays an inordinate amount of its revenue for a copyright license. In short, alternative compensations systems could overcome current impediments to making universal catalogues available online. They could also drastically reduce licensing costs and the considerable burdens of copyright enforcement. Finally, alternative compensation systems prevent powerful social media platforms and other Internet intermediaries from obtaining exclusive licenses to distribute vast catalogues of copyrighted content.

Alternative compensation systems might well be feasible for digital home entertainment markets. In a study published in 2003, I estimated that a levy of just over 4 percent on goods and services used to trade files of copyrighted music recordings, videos, and computer games would compensate rights holders for revenues displaced by peer-to-peer file trading.[5] Granted, to estimate the appropriate size of such a levy today would require taking into account the explosive growth of authorized music and video streaming, as well as that of illicit file trading and streaming of movies and TV shows—developments that have transpired since 2003. In that regard, a 2015 empirical study suggests that, in return for free access to a universal catalogue of music, consumers would willingly pay levies on Internet service in amounts sufficient for composers and recording artists to earn as much or more revenue than under the proprietary copyright system.[6]

On the other hand, levies, statutory licenses, and collective licensing carry significant administrative costs. Proceedings before administrative and judicial bodies charged with setting appropriate compulsory license royalties based on a statutory standard consume substantial time and money. They also tend to provide inadequate incentives for rights holders and would-be licensees to provide the honest and accurate information decision-makers need to determine the compulsory license rate. Finally, creators often complain that collective rights management organizations unfairly discriminate in allocating license proceeds among their members and eat up in administrative overhead an inordinate share of funds meant for authors. Any expansion of compulsory and collective licensing requires streamlining and rationalizing the process for setting royalty rates and distributing funds to creators.

Proposals for alternative compensation systems have gained considerably more traction in Europe than in the United States. As noted above, private copying levies, statutory licenses, and mandatory collective licensing are common in Europe. So are government allocations of compulsory license and copying levy proceeds to fund cultural projects rather than to devote the entire amount to paying the creators whose work has been used. Perhaps surprisingly, despite the authors' rights ideology that characterizes European copyright systems, European countries show considerable willingness to view copyright as part of a broader system of public funding for the arts—and to subordinate authors' proprietary rights in doing so.

By contrast, many stakeholders, commentators, and government officials in the United States regard statutory licenses and even collective rights management as narrow aberrations from the ideal norm of individualized market bargaining. In their view, statutory licenses are warranted only as temporary measures designed to address specific market failures—when high transaction and enforcement costs make individualized voluntary licensing unfeasible. They advocate terminating statutory licenses—and even dispensing with the compulsory licenses that antitrust consent decrees have imposed on ASCAP and BMI—whenever possible.

In the United States, the ideology of the market obscures the fact that voluntary copyright licensing leaves large holes in the catalogues of cultural and information works to which individuals seek access, resulting in diminished public welfare. Market ideology also ignores statutory licensing's singular capacity to spur new technologies and media for disseminating cultural expression by removing copyright holders' veto over those new uses of their works. While alternative compensation systems are not a panacea for copyright's ills, their costs and benefits should be weighed dispassionately, free from the faith-based market ideology that obscures reasoned, empirical analysis.

How might voluntary licensing be reformed?

The Copyright Office and others have raised the possibility of consolidated or "unitary" collective licensing for music, whereby each collective rights management organization could administer all rights required to disseminate recorded music. Today, music streaming and digital download delivery entail a complex patchwork of statutory and voluntary licenses for both musical compositions and sound recordings. Further, those licenses are administered through several collective rights management organizations. Under the reform proposals, the various rights that need to be cleared through voluntary licensing or compensated through statutory licensing would be merged under one-stop licensing organizations empowered to grant blanket licenses for streaming and distributing digital copies of recorded music.

Recall that recorded music consists of two distinct copyrightable works: the musical composition and the sound recording. Currently, the rights to deliver digital downloads of recorded music are typically administered on a per song and per sound recording basis by, respectively, the music publisher holding the mechanical rights to the musical composition and the record label holding the copyright in the sound recording. The rights to stream musical compositions are typically administered by performance rights organizations (primarily ASCAP and BMI). And the rights to stream sound recordings of music are administered by the individual record labels or, in the case of webcasting, SoundExchange, the collective rights management organization representing the record labels.

A unitary blanket license covering streaming and digital distribution of music compositions and sound recordings would go far to reduce the current gridlock in recorded music licensing by greatly simplifying the licensing process and reducing transaction costs. Proposals for such unitary licensing in the United States generally stop short of the type of mandatory collective licensing common in Europe. In European countries, the law often recognizes a single organization with the power to negotiate on behalf of all creators in a particular sector. By contrast, U.S. proposals typically would allow rights holders to opt out of collective licensing organizations. They also envision several umbrella collective licensing organizations competing for members. And they favor unregulated bargaining for license fees. Alternatively, the Copyright Office has raised the possibility of a hybrid system under which collective licensing organizations and users would voluntarily negotiate to determine agreed-upon licensing rates without regulatory intervention, and once those license rates are agreed upon, they would be binding on all members of the group by operation of law.

Given the anticompetitive market power that unitary collective licensing organizations would most likely obtain, some government regulation would be necessary. At the very least, organizations with the power to negotiate a unitary license would have to be required to offer licenses at reasonable rates to all who wish to obtain one. Further, the greater the freedom of large rights holders to opt out, the greater their ability to engage in strategic holdouts against streaming and digital download services that must provide a full catalogue of musical works to be viable players in the digital marketplace. If copyright law allows those holdouts, unitary licensing will yield few benefits beyond our current dysfunctional system.

Unitary collective licensing, subject to government regulation to ensure nondiscriminatory licenses at reasonable rates, merits serious consideration in other sectors as well. Digital technology makes online platforms featuring universal libraries of books, movies, and television shows both feasible and economically efficient. As I have discussed, the Google Book Search class action litigation resulted in a settlement that would have established a unitary licensing system for Google's mass digitization of books while also giving authors and publishers the possibility of opting out. However, the court determined that such a copyright reform should be the province of Congress, not the courts.

Likewise, unless copyright law stands in the way, the future of video distribution is likely to resemble that of music streaming: online streaming platforms featuring full catalogues of television shows and movies. Unitary collective licensing might be effective in that sector as well. In some countries, collective licensing extends to theatrical exhibitions of films and TV shows in public venues and to the use of literary works and music in television broadcasts. Applying collective licensing to online streaming raises a host of issues, including how it would impact directors, writers, and actors guild agreements. But like the Copyright Act's establishment of SoundExchange to represent the record labels in licensing to webcasters, a single organization to represent all movie and television producers would facilitate the featuring of full video catalogues in online video streaming services.

How should Congress solve the orphan works problem?

Recall that orphan works are works for which the copyright owner is unknown. Today, there are millions of orphan works.

As we have seen, the orphan works problem is of Congress' own making. It results from Congress' (1) enactment of an exceedingly long copyright term; (2) abolition of the requirement that a copyright holder must renew the copyright twenty-eight years from publication to avoid having the work enter the public domain; and (3) failure to require that copyright owners register their works and record transfers of copyright ownership with the Copyright Office.

Traditionally, copyright law requires that someone who wishes to use a copyrighted work in a way that falls within the copyright owner's exclusive rights must obtain the copyright owner's permission in advance of the use. Without that advance permission, the user faces liability for copyright infringement unless and until the time that the copyright owner grants permission. Consequently, those who wish to use orphan works do so at their peril. The user risks liability should the copyright owner come out of the woodwork and sue for copyright infringement.

The orphan works problem can plague a documentary filmmaker who wishes to include archival music, film clips, or images in a historical documentary. It can also impede reissues or sequels of out-of-print novels. More pervasively, the orphan works problem blocks the creation of publicly accessible digital archives of legacy books, sound recordings, photographs, and films that might still be in copyright. Under current copyright law, mass digitization projects risk copyright infringement liability for digitizing and displaying copyright works without obtaining copyright holder permission in advance. Moreover, liability may include an award of statutory damages of up to $150,000 per infringed work, which a court may award to the copyright owner without any proof of any actual harm. Given that substantial risk, even well-heeled Google refrains from making available in Google Book search the full text of legacy books that might still be in copyright.

The Copyright Office has issued two reports that address these problems. The first, issued in 2006, addressed the problem of orphan works generally but not issues of mass digitization. The second, issued in 2011, is styled a "preliminary analysis and discussion document" about the legal issues arising from mass digitization.

The 2006 Orphan Works Report proposed that Congress amend the Copyright Act to provide partial immunity from copyright infringement for using an orphan work in a way that would otherwise infringe copyright. In such cases, copyright owners who identify themselves after the orphan work has been used would be entitled only to limited injunctive relief and "reasonable compensation." In addition, certain noncommercial uses of orphan works would be immune even from a requirement of reasonable compensation, but would be subject to an injunction prohibiting any further use of the work. However, the Copyright Office proposed a significant caveat to those limits on liability for using an orphan work. The limited liability would apply only if the user both performed a "reasonably diligent" search for the current copyright owner prior to making use of the work and provided proper attribution to the work's author when appropriate.

The reasonable diligence requirement makes sense if the prospective user wishes to use a single work, such as to produce a remake of an old movie or issue a reprint of an old book. But the bar for reasonable diligence must be low. Otherwise, no documentary filmmaker or other user could risk incorporating an orphan work in a new work, lest a court find that the user's search for the copyright owner was not "reasonably diligent." In that regard, the Copyright Office could assist both users and copyright owners by creating a voluntary registry featuring up-to-date information regarding copyright ownership in registered works.

In addition, when a user builds upon or incorporates an orphan work in a new work, the copyright owner who later surfaces should be entitled only to reasonable compensation for continued use of the work, based in part on the revenue earned by the new work, not an injunction. Documentary filmmakers who incorporate archival music, film clips, or images could not risk being required to remove them from a completed film should the copyright owner come out of the woodwork and demand an exorbitant copyright license fee, backed by the threat of injunction. The same is true of other authors who build on orphan works in creating new creative expression.

Further, it would be completely infeasible to require an archive engaged in mass digitization of legacy works to employ "reasonable diligence" to attempt to locate thousands or millions of copyright owners. The Copyright Office's 2011 mass digitization discussion document recognizes that the requirement of reasonably diligent search is impractical for many mass digitization projects. It also notes that mass digitization may serve important public benefit objectives, including preserving old works, making such works more accessible to libraries, schools, researchers, and disadvantaged populations, and providing authors and copyright holders of out-of-print works with potential new sources of revenue.

As I have outlined in Chapter V, Congress would do best to enact a statutory license enabling the mass digitization of works first made public more than twenty-eight years ago. The statutory license would allow digital archives to make digital copies only for specified uses, akin to lending a book from the library. The license would apply to all works, whether orphan works or not. But statutory license fees would be collected only for works for which a copyright owner has surfaced.

What are the benefits and costs of strengthening copyright enforcement?

The explosive growth of unlicensed file sharing on a massive, global scale has sparked numerous efforts to strengthen copyright enforcement against individual file traders, file-trading platforms, and commercial pirates.

The recording industry launched the most extensive enforcement action against file sharers. Between 2003 and 2008, it brought copyright infringement lawsuits against some 30,000 individuals. That strategy may have raised public awareness that unlicensed file sharing infringes copyright. But it seems to have been unsuccessful in stemming the file-sharing tide. Since the recording industry abandoned its campaign of lawsuits against individual file sharers, only a couple of firms in the pornography industry have pursued that course of action—and they have apparently done so to extract large settlement payments from individuals who do not want the fact that they have been downloading porn to be a matter of public record.

Instead of suing potential customers, copyright industries generally attempt to shut down file-trading platforms and commercial pirates. They also seek to enlist third parties and the government to assume much of the cost of policing against copyright infringement.

Aggressive lawsuits

The Motion Picture Association of America (MPAA) and its member studios have aggressively sued BitTorrent sites featuring infringing movies and TV shows. In so doing, the MPAA has successfully sued and shut down several leading BitTorrent sites, including LokiTorrent, TorrentSpy, and isoHunt. The MPAA lawsuits also seem to have influenced other site operators to terminate their operations before being sued.

But despite those successes, BitTorrent sites, pirate cyberlockers, and pirate streaming sites continue to operate. Many are based outside the United States. The MPAA has had some success against sites in Canada, New Zealand, Brazil, and other countries, but less so in countries where copyright enforcement is limited or nonexistent. The MPAA regularly provides information on those sites to the U.S. government. However, absent foreign government willingness to shut those sites down, there is little copyright holders can do to thwart that piracy under current copyright law.

Make intermediaries and credit card companies responsible

Given the barriers to enforcing copyright against pirate sites and platforms based in other countries, copyright industries have turned to Congress for new legislation that would impose broad policing obligations on parties with varying degrees of involvement in the online distribution of copyrighted expression. The proposed Stop Online Piracy Act of 2011 (SOPA) would have required service providers, payment processors, online advertisers, search engines, domain registries, and domain name registrars to terminate services, block financial transactions, or block Internet access to any website falling in the category of a "foreign infringing site" or a site "dedicated to theft of U.S. property." Recall that SOPA met with resounding defeat in the wake of public protests joined by major social media and technology companies. Yet despite SOPA's spectacular demise, then-Register of Copyrights Maria Pallante proclaimed that "the next great Copyright Act presents an opportunity. All members of the online ecosystem should have a role [in copyright enforcement], including payment processors, advertising networks, search engines, Internet service providers, and copyright owners. These strategies can be a mix of legislative solutions and complementary voluntary initiatives, but where gaps in the law exist Congress should not be absent."[7]

Voluntary initiatives

As of this writing, Congress has not enacted a successor to SOPA that would impose obligations to block or withhold financing from foreign-based websites that infringe copyrights. But what of the "voluntary initiatives" that Register Pallante proffered? There has been some movement on that front, but with mixed success.

With the active encouragement of the Obama administration, some "members of the online ecosystem" agreed to voluntary initiatives designed to combat massive copyright infringement. In 2013, major movie studios, record labels, and Internet service providers (ISPs) agreed to institute a voluntary program, viewed as a means to combat piracy without the need for congressional legislation. Under the so-called Copyright Alert System, copyright owners would send notices of alleged copyright infringement to the ISP, which would then forward the notice to its allegedly infringing subscriber in the form of a copyright alert. Under the Copyright Alert System, ISPs would send subscribers up to six alerts, with increasing degrees of seriousness. The first was just an informational notice. The final alert would impose a "Mitigation Measure" of the ISP's choosing, which might include a temporary slowdown of the subscriber's Internet service or redirecting the subscriber's website browsing to a webpage featuring educational information about respecting copyright. ISPs would not be required to terminate recalcitrant subscribers' Internet service.

In 2017, the studios, labels, and ISPs let the Copyright Alert System lapse. The copyright industries expressed frustration that the voluntary program failed to deter hardcore repeat infringers. According to an MPAA statement, those repeat infringers bear primary responsibility for the "estimated 981 million movies and TV shows" downloaded in the United States in 2016 using peer-to-peer file-trading platforms. The copyright industries insist that ISPs should have to do far more to terminate such repeat infringers if ISPs wish to enjoy the ISP safe harbor under the DMCA (which requires that the ISP has "reasonably implemented" a policy to terminate repeat infringers).

Likewise, in 2012 major credit card companies and other payment processors joined with a coalition of copyright and trademark owners called the International AntiCounterfeiting Coalition (IACC) to establish the Payment Processor Initiative & Portal Program, now dubbed "RogueBlock." Program members agree to withhold payment services for illegal transactions, including for sales of pirated materials. Under the Program, rights holders notify payment processors of online merchants engaged in such sales, and payment processors then voluntarily terminate those merchants' accounts. The IACC website claims that "the program has terminated over 5,000 individual counterfeiters' merchant accounts, which has impacted over 200,000 websites."[8] Likewise, in 2015 the U.S. Chamber of Commerce and other organizations launched the Brand Integrity Program, designed to convince advertisers and ad agencies to avoid ad placement on websites that facilitate the distribution of pirated content.

Finally, leading Internet intermediaries, notably Google and Facebook, have voluntarily adopted filtering technologies that block infringing content or enable copyright owners to monetize it. Those filtering systems have been the most successful voluntary measure for copyright enforcement. As I discussed in Chapter V, YouTube's Content ID has largely replaced the DMCA notice and takedown process on YouTube. Further, all but a small fraction of user-posted videos tagged by Content ID remain on YouTube and are monetized by the copyright owner. Nonetheless, such filtering systems also sweep a great deal of noninfringing material in their net. As a result, they enhance copyright enforcement at the risk of suppressing fair use and other noninfringing speech.

Greater criminal penalties and government enforcement

The copyright industry has lobbied aggressively for federal criminal prosecution of peer-to-peer file traders, file-trading platform providers, and illicit storage locker and streaming sites. The industry-supported No Electronic Theft Act of 1997 provides that large-scale file trading can constitute a crime, even if undertaken without any intent to profit monetarily. Likewise, the DMCA provides for criminal penalties for both willfully circumventing technological protection measures and marketing circumvention devices or software.

Thus far, the Department of Justice has generally resisted pressure to bring indictments against individual file sharers and circumventors. To its credit, the DOJ has focused almost entirely on commercial pirates, websites, and platform providers. Notably, in January 2012 the DOJ brought a felony indictment against the popular online storage locker Megaupload and its founder, Kim Dotcom. In February 2017, the New Zealand High Court ruled that Dotcom could be extradited to the United States.

In parallel, the Prioritizing Resources and Organization for Intellectual Property Act of 2008 (PRO-IP Act) provides for enhanced civil remedies and criminal sanctions, grants greater funding and resources for several federal enforcement programs, and creates the position of the Intellectual Property Enforcement Coordinator within the Executive Office of the President. More recently, the Register of Copyrights called for making large-scale, willful, for-profit streaming of infringing television programs, movies, and music a felony. The Register's proposal would thus subject infringing streaming to a criminal penalty akin to that which now applies to large-scale commercial reproduction and distribution of pirated copies. The Obama administration also recommended legislation that would provide for greater criminal penalties for persons previously convicted of criminal copyright infringement.

While arguably effective in curtailing commercial piracy, federal government anti-piracy initiatives have fueled concerns about the potential burdens on civil liberty and free expression that criminal copyright enforcement might impose. Under "Operation in Our Sites," for example, the Immigration and Customs Enforcement arm of the Department of Homeland Security has shut down and seized the domain names of hundreds of websites allegedly involved in online infringement. It has done so without any adversarial hearing—indeed, without even providing notice to affected parties until weeks or months later. Users seeking to visit the targeted websites are redirected to a website bearing the seals of U.S. government enforcement agencies. The Department of Homeland Security has seized the domain names pursuant to PRO-IP Act provisions providing that any property used to commit or facilitate infringement of intellectual property rights is subject to forfeiture to the U.S. government. Operation in Our Sites has resulted in much-publicized erroneous seizures of domain names of noninfringing websites, thus abridging the website proprietors' free speech and due process rights.

Summary

Initiatives to ratchet up copyright enforcement include increasing taxpayer-funded criminal enforcement, requiring Internet intermediaries to block access to foreign websites identified as infringing, and requiring Internet intermediaries to police users' copyright infringement on their own sites and platforms. Copyright law reformers should assess the costs, burdens on civil liberties, and overall effectiveness of those measures. In particular, policy makers must weigh the costs and effectiveness of greater enforcement against that of alternative compensation systems. As discussed above, such systems would provide copyright holders with revenues from statutory licenses and levies rather than seeking to enforce proprietary copyright through civil litigation or creating an expansive apparatus of federal criminal enforcement.

What about authorship credit in the digital arena?

Authors of all stripes, even those who are happy to have their work disseminated for free, generally care greatly about being given authorship credit for their creative expression. Many authors also feel deeply affronted when others modify their work without permission. Yet our online culture is replete with remixing, repurposing, and redistributing creative works with neither credit given to the original author nor permission granted for modifying the author's work. Perhaps even worse, a remix might grossly distort an author's original work without disclaiming the original author's involvement.

Digital technology should be able to provide at least a partial remedy to those problems without unduly restricting the dynamism and freedom of remix culture that many celebrate.

Remixes and modified versions of authors' works could be accompanied by a hypertext link to an unaltered and readily accessible copy of the original. That practice would serve to accord authorship credit for the underlying work, avoid confusion regarding which is the "authentic" copyright-holder-authorized version, and refer interested persons to the underlying work so they can see what has been changed.

Indeed, it might not even be necessary for the remixer to add a hypertext link. Digital technology enables authors to embed authorship and copyright ownership information, as well as licensing information, in digital copies of their work. The DMCA prohibits the intentional removal or alteration of such "copyright management information."

The copyright management information regime provides the best solution to authorship credit in the digital arena. If the author of a work values authorship credit sufficiently, he or she can embed copyright management information identifying the author in digital copies of the work. Or creators can bargain with their publisher, studio, or label to include that information. The DMCA would then require users to retain the copyright management information in digital copies of the work. Retaining copyright management information should also be recognized as a relevant factor for determining whether a reuse qualifies as a fair use or whether the user qualifies for the benefit of statutory licensing.

Whatever the solution, precise requirements should depend on context, following a reasonableness standard rather than a hard-and-fast rule. Authorship attribution requirements might be eased for noncommercial uses or settings that render the original source obvious to all readers and viewers, such as fan fiction websites.

Can copyright reform be achieved by private party agreements rather than legislation?

Industry stakeholders and nonprofit associations have increasingly turned to private ordering as a means to ameliorate what they view as the major shortcomings of copyright law. Proponents tout private ordering as a highly useful tool for bringing parties together to resolve ongoing battles over copyright to the benefit of all involved. Further, private party agreements avoid the difficulty of getting copyright reform legislation through Congress and the uncertainty of judicial interpretation of the Copyright Act. Critics express concern that private ordering arrangements leave out protections for the public at large. Industry-wide agreements also sidestep fundamental features of our constitutional system of government, including lawmaking by elected representatives and protection for individuals under principles of due process and the First Amendment.

I have already touched upon several examples of private ordering. Google, the Authors Guild, and several major publishers effectively created a private compulsory license regime in their proposed settlement of the copyright infringement class action litigation over the Google Books Library Project. The settlement would have enabled Google to scan and display the entire text of in-copyright books unless the copyright owner opted out. The court rejected the proposed settlement. It held that the parties had structured an arrangement that reached substantially beyond the matters in dispute in the copyright infringement lawsuit (whether Google's scanning and display of short snippets is fair use), supplanted the role of Congress, and favored one copyright user—Google—at the expense of others who might wish to engage in mass digitization of books.

Two additional examples of private ordering include the Copyright Alert System and Payment Processor Initiative & Portal Program, which Internet service providers and payment processors agreed to institute with active encouragement from copyright industries and the Obama administration. Another example is Internet service providers' deployment of automated systems to flag user postings that copyright owner-supplied metadata identify as infringing. These arrangements have aimed to resolve disputes over Internet intermediaries' and payment processors' responsibility for policing copyright infringement. Although courts have thus far generally refused to impose policing obligations on Internet intermediaries, private ordering serves the intermediaries' interest in staving off legislative amendments to the Internet service provider safe harbor provisions and in maintaining working relations with the copyright industries. At the same time, the Copyright Alert System was recently abandoned by the parties, demonstrating the potential fragility of private ordering.

Other private ordering examples abound. The following are three more worth mentioning.

Creative Commons

Creative Commons is a nonprofit organization devoted to expanding the universe of creative works available for others to build upon legally and to share. To achieve this goal, Creative Commons uses several standard copyright licenses—each associated with a visual symbol—through which authors can communicate to the public which rights they reserve and which they waive with respect to the work covered by the Creative Commons license. For example, the Creative Commons Attribution-Share Alike License allows others to remix, tweak, and build upon the author's work, whether for noncommercial or commercial purposes—as long as the user credits the author and licenses any new, derivative creations under the identical terms. Other Creative Commons licenses forbid commercial uses or making changes in the work and/or do not impose the share-alike condition. Creative Commons views its public licenses as an adjunct to copyright law reform, not a substitute. As its website states: "Our licenses will always provide voluntary options for creators who wish to share their material on more open terms than current copyright systems allow. But the CC vision—universal access to research and education and full participation in culture—will not be realized through licensing alone."

Best practice statements and fair use

With the assistance of copyright law experts, a number of associations representing users of copyrighted materials (some of whom are also creators) have issued best practice statements setting out their view of the types of uses that would clearly qualify as fair use. Prominent examples include the Documentary Filmmakers' Statement of Best Practices in Fair Use, the Dance Heritage Coalition's Statement of Best Practices in Fair Use of Dance-Related Materials, and the Society for Cinema and Media Studies' Statement of Best Practices in Fair Use in Teaching for Film and Media Educators. The best practice statements are meant to achieve greater certainty for users than does fair use case law. Recall that fair use depends on judges' application of four statutory factors, in addition to other possible factors of the court's making, on a case-by-case basis. As a result, the best practices are generally more restrictive than some judicial interpretations of fair use doctrine might support. For example, the Documentary Filmmakers' Statement of Best Practices in Fair Use states that it should generally be fair use for a filmmaker to quote works of popular culture to illustrate a point the filmmaker is developing. But the statement cautions that filmmakers should properly attribute the works they quote and should draw from a range of different sources, neither of which is necessarily required to qualify for fair use. In some cases, best practice statements are also intended to encourage insurance companies to issue errors and omissions insurance for projects, such as documentary films, that comply with the best practices set out in the statement.

Further, the best practice statements are meant to influence judges' fair use analysis to the extent that judicial determinations of fair use explicitly or implicitly depend on general norms and practices in certain industries. Nonetheless, there is no guarantee that a court would adopt the same understanding of fair use as set out in an applicable best practice statement. Indeed, the best practice statements are typically issued by a users' association without explicit copyright industry agreement that the statement's view of fair use is acceptable to copyright holders. As of this writing, such statements have yet to be tested in court.

While best practice statements have been issued mostly by user associations in recent years, a set of fair use guidelines drafted by publishers and authors and incorporated into the legislative history of the Copyright Act of 1976 seems to have had the most far-reaching influence. The Agreement on Guidelines for Classroom Copying in Not-for-Profit Educational Institutions was meant to effect a compromise between publishers and authors, on one side, and educational institutions, on the other. However, it seems to have been crafted with minimal input from educators. Indeed, the Classroom Guidelines were adopted over the express opposition of the American Association of University Professors and the Association of American Law Schools, which claimed that the Guidelines were unduly restrictive of classroom copying and instruction. The Guidelines were meant to set out a safe harbor for classroom copying—copying practices that undoubtedly qualify as fair use, not the maximum extent of copying that might so qualify. But some courts—and university administrators—have viewed the Guidelines as delimiting the maximum parameters of fair use in the classroom copying context.

Open access

University professors generate numerous articles that appear in peer-reviewed scholarly and scientific journals published by commercial publishers such as Elsevier, Springer, and Sage. In recent years commercial publishers of such academic journals have dramatically increased the prices they charge, primarily to university libraries, for subscriptions to journal content—this even though both authors and peer reviewers of academic articles typically provide their services and work product without compensation from the journal. As a result, universities and public institutions have begun to push back against commercial publishers' control of academic publications. A number of leading universities have instituted open access policies. The policies require professors to make their work available on free, open access websites or journals, generally within twelve months of publication in a commercial journal, unless the commercial journal objects.

For example, under the University of California's open access policy, "each Faculty member grants to the University of California a nonexclusive, irrevocable, worldwide license to exercise any and all rights under copyright related to each of his or her scholarly articles, in any medium, and to authorize others to do the same, for the purpose of making their articles widely and freely available in an open access registry." In turn, the University of California's open access registry, eScholarship, makes all material in the registry available worldwide, free of cost, to researchers and the general public. Yet, visitors to the eScholarship website are not necessarily free to reprint articles they find on the site. It depends on the article's author. When a faculty member deposits an article with eScholarship, the faculty member may reserve all of his copyright or may select any of a menu of Creative Commons licenses. University of California faculty may withhold articles from eScholarship only if the journal in which they publish refuses to grant permission. But in the face of considerable pressure brought by the university community, most journals agree to open access following a six to twelve month waiting period (or "embargo") following journal publication.

While universities' open access policies fall within the rubric of private ordering, they have drawn inspiration from congressional legislation. Congress enacted an open access policy with respect to publications that report on research funded by the National Institutes of Health (NIH). The Omnibus Appropriations Act of 2009 provides that the Director of the NIH must require "that all investigators funded by the NIH submit or have submitted for them to the National

Library of Medicine's PubMed Central an electronic version of their final, peer-reviewed manuscripts upon acceptance for publication, to be made publicly available no later than 12 months after the official date of publication: Provided, that the NIH shall implement the public access policy in a manner consistent with copyright law." To comply with copyright law, the NIH makes consent to its open access policy a condition of receiving NIH funding and advises authors to "avoid signing any agreements with publishers that do not allow the author to comply with the NIH Public Access Policy."

The Association of American Publishers has lobbied for legislation that would reverse the NIH's public access requirement. Indeed, the publishers' proposed legislation would affirmatively prohibit open access to any research results paid for with tax dollars. Thus far, Congress has not enacted such legislation.

What are the prospects for copyright reform?

To this observer, it seems quite unlikely that Congress will enact a comprehensive copyright revision in the near future. In previous copyright law revisions, Congress has looked to affected industries to hammer out compromises for congressional enactment. But the uncertainty in markets for creative expression wrought by digital technology has greatly raised the stakes of any legislative fiat. As a result, the affected industries have been pulled farther apart. Even when industries have agreed to work together to reduce piracy (or monetize user postings of infringing content)—YouTube's implementation of Content ID filtering is one example—they continue to spar bitterly over what should be the legal rule when there is no such cooperation.

Further, as evidenced by the public outcry over SOPA, social media have given voice and power to millions of individual Internet users who previously had no seat at the bargaining table. Social media also amplifies the voice of individual authors, independently from the copyright industries and collective management organizations that purport to represent them. That public input laudably enhances the democratic process. But, for better or for worse, it makes deal-making among the affected industries more difficult and thus legislated copyright reform less likely.

Given these developments, several reform proposals in recent years have failed to move through Congress. In addition to SOPA, failures include proposals to remedy the problem of orphan works, rationalize music licensing, update statutory license regimes, and enable mass digitization. That track record does not bode well for comprehensive legislative copyright reform even if key stakeholders have recently agreed on proposed legislation to remedy some of the barriers to music licensing.

Nonetheless, the principal copyright reform proposals loom large in the debates over copyright law and policy. And it is possible that, despite recent congressional paralysis on copyright issues (and many other issues), one or more reform proposals will eventually be taken up by Congress. After all, our previous comprehensive copyright law revision was almost two decades in the making before culminating in enactment of the Copyright Act of 1976. Further, as I have discussed, some reform proposals might also be implemented through stakeholders' agreements and other private ordering even in the absence of congressional action.

What should copyright reform aim to accomplish?

No matter what its particulars, copyright reform should aim to further our copyright law's overriding objective: to promote the creation and widespread dissemination of original expression from a diversity of sources. Copyright's exclusive rights can serve as important tools to that end. But broader and longer exclusive rights are not necessarily better. Fair use and copyright's limited duration also serve copyright's purpose. So would alternative compensation systems for universal digital libraries. Unless copyrights are punctuated by such exceptions and limitations, incumbent industries too readily exploit copyright law to stifle new media competition. And while many authors feel affronted when their creative work is used without their permission, building upon the works of others is a time-honored feature of the creative process. It would stifle creativity to prevent authors from remixing, sampling, and otherwise building upon the works of their predecessors as raw material for new expression.

Where possible, then, copyrights should be tailored to providing the economic incentives needed to spur the creation and dissemination of those works that require significant investments of money and time to create. Copyright law should be neutral regarding which creators and industries participate in that endeavor.

NOTES

Chapter I

1. A helpful chart summarizing the various provisions and factual scenarios is Peter B. Hirtle, *Copyright Term and the Public Domain in the United States* (Jan. 1, 2013), http://copyright.cornell.edu/resources/publicdomain.cfm. [Perma Link: http://perma.cc/0yh9BhocjY7.]
2. Sony Corp. of America v. Universal City Studios, Inc., 464 U.S. 417, 477 (1984).
3. MEREDITH ROSE ET AL., CAPTURED: SYSTEMIC BIAS AT THE U.S. COPYRIGHT OFFICE: A PUBLIC KNOWLEDGE REPORT (2016); JESSICA LITMAN, DIGITAL COPYRIGHT 74 (Prometheus Books 2016) (noting that the "Copyright Office has tended to view copyright owners as its real constituency").
4. Peter Pan Fabrics, Inc. v. Martin Weiner Corp., 274 F.2d 487, 489 (2nd Cir. 1960).
5. U.S. Department of Justice, Statement of the Department of Justice on the Closing of the Antitrust Division's Review of the ASCAP and BMI Consent Decrees (Aug. 14, 2016).
6. Bill Rosenblatt, *Proposed Settlement in Spotify Lawsuit Points the Way Towards Solving Music Industry Data Problems*, COPYRIGHT AND TECHNOLOGY, June 5, 2017.
7. U.S. COPYRIGHT OFFICE, COPYRIGHT AND THE MUSIC MARKETPLACE: A REPORT OF THE REGISTER OF COPYRIGHTS (Feb. 2015).
8. Authors Guild, Inc. v. Google Inc., 954 F. Supp. 2d 282, 291 (S.D.N.Y. 2013), affirmed, 804 F.3d 202 (2nd Cir. 2015).

9. 17 U.S.C. § 801(B).

10. *See* Christopher Buccafusco and Paul J. Heald, *Do Bad Things Happen When Works Enter the Public Domain?: Empirical Tests of Copyright Term Extension*, 28 BERKELEY TECH. L.J. 1 (2013) (finding that audiobooks made from public domain bestsellers (1913–22) are significantly more available than those made from copyrighted bestsellers (1923–32)); Paul Heald, *Property Rights and the Efficient Exploitation of Copyrighted Works: An Empirical Analysis of Public Domain and Copyrighted Fiction Bestsellers*, 92 MINN. L. REV. 1031 (2007–2008); Mark A. Lemley, *Ex Ante Versus Ex Post Justifications for Intellectual Property*, 71 U. CHI. L. REV. 129, 136 (2004).

11. U.S. Copyright Office Notice of Inquiry, Study on Moral Rights of Attribution and Integrity, 82 Fed. Reg. 7870 (Jan. 23, 2017).

12. Capitol Records Inc. v. Thomas-Rasset, 680 F. Supp. 2d 1045, 1051 (D. Minn. 2010), citing H.R. Rep. No. 106–216, at 6 (1999).

13. *Google Transparency Report*, https://www.google.com/transparencyreport/removals/copyright/ [Perma link: https://perma.cc/49PX-38P2] (reporting on takedown notices worldwide, not just those sent under the DMCA).

Chapter II

1. CORY DOCTOROW, INFORMATION DOESN'T WANT TO BE FREE: LAWS FOR THE INTERNET AGE (McSweeney's 2014).

2. Katherine Oyama, *Google Senior Policy Counsel, Continuing to Create Value While Fighting Piracy: An Update*, GOOGLE BLOG (July 13, 2016), https://www.blog.google/topics/public-policy/continuing-to-create-value-while/. [Perma link: https://www.blog.google/topics/public-policy/continuing-to-create-value-while.]

3. DAVID PRICE, SIZING THE PIRACY UNIVERSE (NetNames 2013), available at https://www.netnames.com/assets/shared/whitepaper/pdf/netnames-sizing-piracy-universe-FULLreport-sept2013.pdf. [Perma link: https://perma.cc/TC8B-6UCC.]

4. CORY DOCTOROW, INFORMATION DOESN'T WANT TO BE FREE: LAWS FOR THE INTERNET AGE (McSweeney's 2014).

5. JENNIFER M. URBAN, JOE KARAGANIS, AND BRIANNA L. SCHOFIELD, NOTICE AND TAKEDOWN IN EVERYDAY PRACTICE 87–96 (American Assembly 2016).

6. Joel Waldfogel, *And the Bands Played On: Digital Disintermediation and the Quality of Recorded Music* (June 25, 2012), at 4, available

at SSRN: https://papers.ssrn.com/sol3/papers.cfm?abstract_id=2117372.
7. 537 U.S. 186 (2003).
8. Amy Harmon, *A Corporate Victory, But One That Raises Public Consciousness*, N.Y. TIMES, Jan. 16, 2003, at A24.

Chapter III

1. STEPHEN E. SIWEK, COPYRIGHT INDUSTRIES IN THE U.S. ECONOMY: THE 2016 REPORT (2016), at 2.
2. *Id.* at 2, 14.
3. ECONOMICS AND STATISTICS ADMINISTRATION AND THE USPTO, INTELLECTUAL PROPERTY AND THE U.S. ECONOMY: INDUSTRIES IN FOCUS (March 2012); DEPARTMENT OF COMMERCE INTERNET POLICY TASK FORCE, COPYRIGHT POLICY, CREATIVITY, AND INNOVATION IN THE DIGITAL ECONOMY (July 2013).
4. STEPHEN E. SIWEK, COPYRIGHT INDUSTRIES IN THE U.S. ECONOMY: THE 2014 REPORT (2014), Table A.5, at 20 (setting forth breakdown per year for 2009 through 2013). The IIPA did not issue a copyright industries report in 2015, and its 2016 report no longer breaks down exports by copyright industry.
5. *See* BSA/Software Alliance, Public Comment on Copyright Office Section 512 Study, Apr. 1, 2016.
6. TELECOMMUNICATIONS INDUSTRY ASSOCIATION, TIA 2013 PLAYBOOK 31 (2013).
7. STEPHEN E. SIWEK, MEASURING THE U.S. INTERNET SECTOR (Internet Association Dec. 2015), at 5.
8. COMPUTER & COMMUNICATIONS INDUSTRY ASSOCIATION, FAIR USE IN THE U.S. ECONOMY (2017).
9. U.S. GOV'T ACCOUNTABILITY OFFICE, INTELLECTUAL PROPERTY: INSIGHTS GAINED FROM EFFORTS TO QUANTIFY THE EFFECTS OF COUNTERFEIT AND PIRATED GOODS IN THE U.S. ECONOMY (June 9, 2013), at 9–10.
10. *See, for example*, ABRAHAM DRASSINOWER, WHAT'S WRONG WITH COPYING? (Harvard Univ. Press 2015) and Seana Valentine Shiffrin, *Lockean Arguments for Private Intellectual Property, in* NEW ESSAYS IN THE LEGAL AND POLITICAL THEORY OF PROPERTY (Stephen Munzer ed., Cambridge Univ. Press 2001).

Chapter IV

1. Cariou v. Prince, 714 F.3d 694, 708 (2nd Cir. 2013).

Chapter V

1. JOE KARAGANIS AND LENNART RENKEMA, COPY CULTURE IN THE U.S. AND GERMANY 5 (American Assembly 2013).
2. Brett Danaher and Joel Waldfogel, Reel Piracy: The Effect of Online Film Piracy on International Box Office Sales (Jan. 16, 2012), available at SSRN: https://papers.ssrn.com/sol3/papers.cfm?abstract_id=1986299.
3. MARTIN VAN DER ENDE ET AL., ESTIMATING DISPLACEMENT RATES OF COPYRIGHTED CONTENT IN THE EU: FINAL REPORT (European Commission May 2015).
4. Id. at 14.
5. RECORDING INDUSTRY ASSOCIATION OF AMERICA, NEWS AND NOTES ON 2017 MID-YEAR RIAA REVENUE STATISTICS (Sept. 20, 2017) (reporting on significant industry growth—with music streaming revenues accounting for 62 percent of the total market—even if overall market revenues remain below 1999 levels); Ben Sisario, Milestone for BMI: More Than $1 Billion in Music Royalties, N.Y. TIMES (Sept. 8, 2107); Spencer Kornhaber, How Significant Is the Music Industry's Rebound? THE ATLANTIC, Apr. 3, 2017; James Titcomb, Internet Piracy Falls to Record Lows Amid Rise of Spotify and Netflix, THE TELEGRAPH (July 5, 2016) (reporting on UK Intellectual Property Office-commissioned study, Kantar Media, Infringement Levels March—May 2016 (June 2016)).
6. Steven James Watson, Daniel John Zizzo, and Piers Fleming, Determinants of Unlawful File Sharing: A Scoping Review, 10(6) PLoS ONE (June 1, 2015): e0127921. https://doi.org/10.1371/journal.pone.0127921. [Perma link: https://doi.org/10.1371/journal.pone.0127921.]
7. MARTIN VAN DER ENDE ET AL., ESTIMATING DISPLACEMENT RATES OF COPYRIGHTED CONTENT IN THE EU: FINAL REPORT 162–63 (European Commission May 2015).
8. Felix Oberholzer-Gee & Koleman Strumpf, File Sharing and Copyright, in 10 INNOVATION POLICY AND THE ECONOMY 48–49 (Josh Lerner & Scott Stern eds., 2010); Split Screens: A Tale of Two Tinseltowns, THE ECONOMIST, Feb. 23, 2013.
9. STEPHEN E. SIWEK, COPYRIGHT INDUSTRIES IN THE U.S. ECONOMY: THE 2016 REPORT 7–8 (2016); STEPHEN E. SIWEK, COPYRIGHT INDUSTRIES IN THE U.S. ECONOMY: THE 2014 REPORT 5–10 (2014); STEPHEN E. SIWEK, COPYRIGHT INDUSTRIES IN THE U.S. ECONOMY: THE 2013 REPORT 9–10 (2013); STEPHEN E. SIWEK,

Copyright Industries in the U.S. Economy: The 2011 Report 5 (2011); Stephen E. Siwek, Copyright Industries in the U.S. Economy: The 2003–2007 Report 5 (2009).

10. Ian Hargreaves et al., Digital Opportunity: A Review of Intellectual Property and Growth (2011).

11. Katherine Oyama, Google Senior Policy Counsel, *Continuing to Create Value While Fighting Piracy: An Update*, Google Blog (July 13, 2016), https://www.blog.google/topics/public-policy/continuing-to-create-value-while/. [Perma link: https://www.blog.google/topics/public-policy/continuing-to-create-value-while.]

12. Recording Industry Association of America, *Five Stubborn Truths about YouTube and the Value Gap*, Medium Blog (Aug. 18, 2017), https://medium.com/@RIAA/five-stubborn-truths-about-youtube-and-value-gap-4faff133271f. [Perma link: https://medium.com/@RIAA/five-stubborn-truths-about-youtube-and-value-gap-4faff133271f.]

13. Lyor Cohen, *Five Observations From My Time at YouTube*, YouTube Official Blog (Aug. 17, 2017), https://youtube.googleblog.com/2017/08/five-observations-from-my-time-at.html. [Perma link: https://perma.cc/4WNF-6EGN.]

14. Students of law and economics will recognize the Coasean ideal that in a competitive market without transaction cost impediments, parties will bargain to achieve the economically efficient result regardless of how the law initially allocates rights between them.

15. Lucas Shaw, YouTube, Music Labels, End Standoff, Move Toward Paid Service, Bloomberg, December 19, 2017, https://www.bloomberg.com/news/articles/2017-12-19/youtube-pacts-with-universal-sony-music-to-allow-paid-service.

16. Statement to the Associated Press (November 2003), as quoted in *DVD-Copy Program Tweaked After Court Order*, CNN.com (Feb. 23, 2004).

17. Motion Picture Association of America, Comments on United States Copyright Office Section 512 Study (Apr. 1, 2016), at 4.

18. For illuminating discussion of this point, see Matthew Sag, *Internet Safe Harbors and the Transformation of Copyright Law*, 93 Notre Dame L. Rev. (forthcoming 2017).

19. Comments of the Recording Industry Association of America, Inc., Before the United States Copyright Office, In the Matter of

Music Licensing Study: Notice and Request for Public Comment (May 23, 2014), at 8.

20. Gary Myer, *The Future of TV Isn't Apps: We Need All Our Channels in One Place*, WIRED (June 2014), http://www.wired.com/2014/06/future-tv-is-not-apps.

21. Fox Television Stations, Inc. v. Aereokiller LLC, 851 F.3d 1002 (9th Cir. 2017).

22. Derek Thompson, *Why the "End of TV" Is Great for Facebook and Google*, THE ATLANTIC, June 2, 2017.

23. U.S. Copyright Office, Legal Issues in Mass Digitization: A Preliminary Analysis and Discussion Document (October 2011).

Chapter VI

1. For a highly informative account of U.S. efforts to enshrine its digital agenda in a new treaty, see Pamela Samuelson, *The U.S. Digital Agenda at WIPO*, 37 VIRGINIA J. INT'L L. 369 (1997).

Chapter VII

1. Jessica D. Litman, *Copyright, Compromise, and Legislative History*, 72 CORNELL L. REV. 857 (1987).

2. Maria A. Pallante, *The Next Great Copyright Act*, 36 COLUM. J.L. & ARTS 315 (2013).

3. Pamela Samuelson and Members of the CPP, *The Copyright Principles Project: Directions for Reform*, 25 BERKELEY TECH. L. J. 1175 (2010).

4. Peter Roff, *The Internet Is Not the Wild West*, U.S. NEWS & WORLD REPORT, July 23, 2013, http://www.usnews.com/opinion/blogs/peter-roff/2013/07/23/congress-must-reform-copyright-law-for-the-digital-age.

5. Neil Weinstock Netanel, *Impose a Noncommercial Use Levy to Allow Free Peer-to-Peer File Trading*, 17 HARV. J.L. & TECH. 1 (2003).

6. See João Pedro Quintais, ALTERNATIVE COMPENSATION MODELS FOR LARGE-SCALE NON-COMMERCIAL ONLINE USES (2015) (discussing Dutch study), available at SSRN: https://papers.ssrn.com/sol3/papers.cfm?abstract_id=2625492.

7. Maria A. Pallante, *The Next Great Copyright Act*, 36 COLUM. J.L. & ARTS 315, 326 (2013).

8. IACC, *IACC RogueBlock®* (June 19, 2017), http://www.iacc.org/online-initiatives/rogueblock. [Perma link: http://www.iacc.org/online-initiatives/rogueblock.]

FURTHER READING

Cameron, Lisa, and Coleman Bazelon. *The Impact of Digitization on Business Models in Copyright-Driven Industries: A Review of the Economic Issues.* U.S. National Research Council, 2013, available at http://files.brattle.com/files/6705_the_impact_of_digitization_on_business_models_in_copyright-driven_industries_cameron_bazelon_feb_26_2013.pdf.

Doctorow, Cory. *Information Doesn't Want to Be Free: Laws for the Internet Age.* San Francisco: McSweeney's, 2014.

Elkin-Koren, Niva. "Tailoring Copyright to Social Production." *Theoretical Inquiries in Law* 12 (2011): 309–347.

Fisher, William W., III. *Promises to Keep: Technology, Law, and the Future of Entertainment.* Stanford, CA: Stanford University Press, 2004.

Ginsburg, Jane C. "Moral Rights in the U.S.: Still in Need of a Guardian Ad Litem." *Cardozo Arts & Entertainment Law Journal* 30, no. 1 (2012): 73–90.

———. "Fair Use for Free, or Permitted-but-Paid?" *Berkeley Technology Law Journal* 29, no. 3 (2014): 1383–1446.

Hargreaves, Ian, et al. *Digital Opportunity: A Review of Intellectual Property and Growth.* 2011, available at https://www.gov.uk/government/uploads/system/uploads/attachment_data/file/32563/ipreview-finalreport.pdf. [Perma link: https://perma.cc/YQW5-X5JK.]

Litman, Jessica. *Digital Copyright.* Amherst, NY: Prometheus Books, 2001.

Menell, Peter S. "Adapting Copyright for the Mashup Generation." *University of Pennsylvania Law Review* 164 (2016): 441–512.

National Research Council of the National Academies. *Copyright in the Digital Era: Building Evidence for Policy.* Edited by Stephen A. Merrill and William J. Raduchel. Washington, DC: National Academies Press, 2013.

Netanel, Neil W. *Copyright's Paradox.* New York: Oxford University Press, 2008.

Nimmer, David. "Codifying Copyright Comprehensibly." *UCLA Law Review* 51, no. 5 (2004): 1233–1387.

Okediji, Ruth L., ed. *Copyright Law in an Age of Limitations and Exceptions.* New York: Cambridge University Press, 2017.

Pallante, Maria A. "The Next Great Copyright Act." *Columbia Journal of Law & Arts* 36, no. 3 (2013): 315–344.

Patry, William. *Moral Panics and the Copyright Wars.* New York: Oxford University Press, 2009.

Samuelson, Pamela, and Members of the CPP. "The Copyright Principles Project: Directions for Reform." *Berkeley Technology Law Journal* 25, no. 3 (2010): 1175–1245.

Urban, Jennifer M., Brianna L. Schofield, and Joe Karaganis. *Notice and Takedown in Everyday Practice.* New York: American Assembly, 2016.

U.S. Copyright Office. *Report on Orphan Works.* Washington, DC, 2006.

———. *Legal Issues in Mass Digitization: A Preliminary Analysis and Discussion Document.* Washington, DC, 2011.

———. *Copyright and the Music Marketplace.* Washington, DC, 2015.

U.S. Department of Commerce Internet Policy Task Force. *Copyright Policy, Creativity, and Innovation in the Digital Economy.* Washington, DC, 2013.

U.S. Government Accountability Office. *Insights Gained from Efforts to Quantify the Effects of Counterfeit and Pirated Goods in the U.S. Economy.* Washington, DC: U.S. Government Accountability Office, 2013.

Waldfogel, Joel. "Copyright Research in the Digital Age: Moving from Piracy to the Supply of New Products." *American Economic Review, Papers and Proceedings* 102, no. 3 (May 2012): 337–342.

———. "Copyright Protection, Technological Change, and the Quality of New Products: Evidence from Recorded Music since Napster." *Journal of Law & Economics* 55, no. 4 (November 2012): 715–740.

INDEX

and Copyright Royalty Board,
18, 37, 40, 42, 141
and foreign authors/works,
167–168
and Google Books Library
Project, 159
and mechanical, 38
and mobile TV, 154
and public performance, 32–33
and record labels, 76, 119
and sound recordings, 44
streaming, 78, 143–145
and YouTube, 136

safe harbor. *See* DMCA;
Hollywood: versus Silicon
Valley; Internet service
provider
sampling, digital, 21, 82, 103,
125–126, 205. *See also* remix
culture
satellite television. *See*
television: cable and
satellite
search engine, 63, 65, 100, 133,
158, 179
and advertising revenue, 78, 93
and copyright enforcement,
73–74, 192
and Google Books, 158–159
and notice and takedown,
58–59, 75
and safe harbor, 55–58
and voluntary
agreements, 65–66
Second Circuit Court of Appeals,
134, 152, 158
secondary liability. *See*
infringement
SESAC (Society of European
Stage Authors and
Composers), 33
Shakespeare, 23–24, 46, 63, 127

sharing. *See* file sharing; remix
culture
Silicon Valley, 63–66, 82–83
social media platforms, 70,
116–120, 183. *See also*
Facebook; YouTube
and filtering technologies,
137–140
and infringement, 133–137
Software. *See* computer software
*Sony Corp. v. Universal City
Studios*, 85–86, 103–104,
131–133, 150, 155. *See also*
fair use doctrine
SOPA (Stop Online Piracy Act),
xvi, 192, 203–204
sound recording, 28–31, 36–
37, 42, 186. *See also*
licensing; remix culture;
SoundExchange
SoundExchange, 181, 186, 187.
See also collective rights
management
organization
space-shifting, 104–105,
128–129, 155. *See also* fair
use doctrine
Spotify, 62, 76, 108–109, 122. *See
also* webcaster
and music licensing, 34–39, 64
and YouTube, 118–119
stakeholders, 49, 58, 64, 176, 178
and compulsory and statutory
licenses, 141, 143, 184
and private ordering, 197, 204
"staple article of commerce"
doctrine, 131–133. See also
*Sony Corp. v. Universal City
Studios*
state copyright laws, 10, 29
Statute of Anne of 1710
(UK), 81, 85
statutory damages. *See* damages

Printed in the USA/Agawam, MA
September 17, 2018

683455.032